YOR

The Mill
on the Floss

George Eliot

Note by Nicola Griffin

Longman   York Press

Nicola Griffin is hereby identified as author of this work in accordance with
Section 77 of the Copyright, Designs and Patents Act 1988

YORK PRESS
322 Old Brompton Road, London SW5 9JH

PEARSON EDUCATION LIMITED
Edinburgh Gate, Harlow,
Essex CM20 2JE, United Kingdom
Associated companies, branches and representatives throughout the world

First published 1999

ISBN 0–582–38192–4

Designed by Vicki Pacey
Illustrated by Jenny Bidgood
Family tree by G.J. Galsworthy
Phototypeset by Gem Graphics, Trenance, Mawgan Porth, Cornwall
Colour reproduction and film output by Spectrum Colour
Produced by Addison Wesley Longman China Limited, Hong Kong

CONTENTS

PREFACE

York Notes are designed to give you a broader perspective on works of literature studied at GCSE and equivalent levels. We have carried out extensive research into the needs of the modern literature student prior to publishing this new edition. Our research showed that no existing series fully met students' requirements. Rather than present a single authoritative approach, we have provided alternative viewpoints, empowering students to reach their own interpretations of the text. York Notes provide a close examination of the work and include biographical and historical background, summaries, glossaries, analyses of characters, themes, structure and language, cultural connections and literary terms.

If you look at the Contents page you will see the structure for the series. However, there's no need to read from the beginning to the end as you would with a novel, play, poem or short story. Use the Notes in the way that suits you. Our aim is to help you with your understanding of the work, not to dictate how you should learn.

York Notes are written by English teachers and examiners, with an expert knowledge of the subject. They show you how to succeed in coursework and examination assignments, guiding you through the text and offering practical advice. Questions and comments will extend, test and reinforce your knowledge. Attractive colour design and illustrations improve clarity and understanding, making these Notes easy to use and handy for quick reference.

York Notes are ideal for:
- Essay writing
- Exam preparation
- Class discussion

The author of this Note is Nicola Griffin. She received a BA Hons degree at Birmingham University and a PGCE at Chester College. She is currently Head of English at an independent school in Chester and a senior examiner and moderator for a major examination board.

The text used in this Note is *The Mill on the Floss* in the Penguin Popular Classics series.

Health Warning: **This study guide will enhance your understanding, but should not replace the reading of the original text and/or study in class.**

PART ONE

INTRODUCTION

HOW TO STUDY A NOVEL

You have bought this book because you wanted to study a novel on your own. This may supplement classwork.

- You will need to read the novel several times. Start by reading it quickly for pleasure, then read it slowly and carefully. Further readings will generate new ideas and help you to memorise the details of the story.
- Make careful notes on themes, plot and characters of the novel. The plot will change some of the characters. Who changes?
- The novel may not present events chronologically. Does the novel you are reading begin at the beginning of the story or does it contain flashbacks and a muddled time sequence? Can you think why?
- How is the story told? Is it narrated by one of the characters or by an all-seeing ('omniscient') narrator?
- Does the same person tell the story all the way through? Or do we see the events through the minds and feelings of a number of different people?
- Which characters does the narrator like? Which characters do you like or dislike? Do your sympathies change during the course of the book? Why? When?
- Any piece of writing (including your notes and essays) is the result of thousands of choices. No book had to be written in just one way: the author could have chosen other words, other phrases, other characters, other events. How could the author of your novel have written the story differently? If events were recounted by a minor character how would this change the novel?

Studying on your own requires self-discipline and a carefully thought-out work plan in order to be effective. Good luck.

Childhood
This is very similar to Maggie's and Tom's relationship in the book, and they share the same years of birth.

George Eliot was born Mary Ann Evans in 1819, in Warwickshire. Her father was a land agent overseeing an estate in Nuneaton, and she had a sister, Chrissy, born in 1814, and a brother, Isaac, born in 1816, of whom Mary Ann was very fond. She was a plain but intelligent child and her father's favourite, just as Maggie is.

Religion
Note the parallel with Maggie's reaction after reading Thomas à Kempis.

At school she met Maria Lewis, a teacher and firm evangelical (follower of a strongly emotional form of Protestantism). At fifteen Mary Ann experienced a form of conversion to this way of thinking and later rejected the traditional Protestant faith altogether. She refused to attend church with her father, causing a rift between them which never completely healed, although she nursed him until he died.

Her meeting with Lewes

In the 1840s Mary Ann became interested in the biblical criticism of German scholars and translated Strauss's *Life of Christ*. This brought her into contact with the leading intellectuals of the day, such as Herbert Spenser and Harriet Martineau. In 1852 she became assistant editor of the *Westminster Review*, a radical intellectual periodical and through this work met George Lewes, a philosopher and author. In 1854 they visited Germany as husband and wife, although Lewes was married to a woman who refused to divorce him.

The scandal
Notice the similarity to St Ogg's judgement of Maggie and her rift with Tom.

In Victorian times it was considered scandalous for an unmarried couple to live together. On their return from Germany, George and Mary Ann (or Marian Lewes as she now wished to be known) were rejected by Victorian society, and even spat on in the street. Isaac, too, refused all contact with his sister, only writing to her again after Lewes's death in 1878. Despite her grief at being separated from her family Marian was nevertheless very happy and for the next twenty years she and Lewes were inseparable.

The novels   Lewes encouraged her to develop her writing, in particular fiction, and during this period she published her major novels. These included *Scenes from Clerical Life* (1857), *Adam Bede* (1859), *The Mill on the Floss* (1860), *Silas Marner* (1861), *Romola* (1863), *Felix Holt: the Radical* (1866), *Middlemarch* (1871) and *Daniel Deronda* (1876). Because of the prevailing attitudes to women all her work was published under the pen name 'George Eliot', and it is as George Eliot that she will be referred to from now on.

Her death   In 1880, two years after Lewes's death, George Eliot married John Cross, a man twenty years her junior. Only then did Isaac renew contact with his sister, sending a brief note of congratulations on her marriage. She replied in a loving tone which showed how much she had missed him, speaking of her affection for him *Just like Maggie's* 'which began when we were little ones'. She died in *love for Tom.* December 1880, five months after returning from her honeymoon in Europe.

CONTEXT & SETTING

The Victorian era: change and progress   Although George Eliot set *The Mill on the Floss* in 1829, eight years before Victoria became queen, the novel (published in 1860) reflects the attitudes of the Victorian era in which the author lived. There were many social changes during the Victorian era, including:

- Increasing industrialisation and the use of machinery
- Movement of people from the countryside to towns and cities
- Changing attitudes to religion, women and morality

In the book, however, Eliot takes us back to the time of her childhood when these changes were just beginning. In many respects, it can be seen as an **autobiographical novel** (see Literary Terms). It was one of the first novels to focus on the lives of ordinary people and to explore ideas rather than just to entertain (see Language and Style).

The age of machinery

The Victorians were very proud of their progress. This pride is reflected in uncle Deane's comment to Tom 'the world goes on at a smarter pace. It's this steam, you see'. St Ogg's is on the brink of change: the past is shown in the Dodsons' repetitive traditions and out-dated clothes, contrasting with the new prosperity of the Deanes. Dorlcote Mill is a peaceful place, cut off from the 'world beyond' by 'a great curtain of sound' (p. 4), but Maggie seems also to welcome change despite the tragedy it can bring. Certainly she feels restricted by the limited ideas of St Ogg's and she needs to progress to higher things: she is seen as 'thirsty for knowledge' (see Themes).

Look at the lovely description of the Mill in Chapter One.

A changing town, changing fortunes

The community of St Ogg's, where some people welcome and benefit from change (the Guests and the Deanes) while others, unable to adapt, are destroyed (Mr Tulliver), shows Eliot's ideas of how individuals adapt or are destroyed by the changing world around them. Tulliver is the victim of his own character and of changing forces beyond his control. He half-realises this when he seeks to get Tom educated 'so as he might be up to the tricks o' these fellows' (p. 5).

Is man an ape?

Religion was also seen in a new light after the publication of Darwin's *On the Origin of Species* in 1859, which Eliot would have discussed with her intellectual friends. The idea that man had evolved from apes rather than being created by God threw doubts on the basis of Christianity and many intellectuals rejected traditional forms of religion, including Eliot herself.

Like Maggie's changed view after she reads Thomas à Kempis.

A man's world

Victorian society followed strict rules of behaviour, particularly for women – this is shown by St Ogg's rejection of Maggie after the incident with Stephen Guest. When the work was published critics rejected the 'unrealistic' picture of Maggie's behaviour, as the Victorians' male-dominated society would not accept the idea of Maggie acting passionately.

Victorian ladies should be pretty, quiet and not too clever – like Lucy.

Women were seen as inferior to men. Wakem's comment (p. 436), 'We don't ask what a woman does, we ask whom she belongs to' says it all. Eliot had to write under a male name to have her work taken seriously and her picture of the unconventional Maggie challenged current ideas about women.

Why is setting important?

The setting of the story and the time in which it takes place help us understand the character, themes and ideas. Eliot chose a town in Lincolnshire in the 1830s. This is important for several reasons.

Realism

Dorlcote Mill is like Griff House where Eliot grew up.

Eliot went to great lengths researching the right place in Lincolnshire to set her novel: she wanted a place that had a history of flooding to make it **realistic** (see Literary Terms). She drew on her own childhood experiences of the countryside for the setting and her knowledge of **dialect** is clear in Bob Jakin's speech.

Changing times

Eliot chose a typical small town with a long history that was on the brink of change owing to the coming of business and industry: 'one of those old, old towns' which has not yet got 'new-fashioned smartness' (p. 117). This lets her show both the effect of change and the oppression of living in such a limited community.

Maggie the outcast

Is there another character who does not fit convention?

Maggie lives on the outskirts of the town in a mill. By setting her in this small, traditional place, the author helps us to understand the problems caused by her unconventional character (see Characters). St Ogg's rejects her as she does not fit into the expected pattern of behaviour for a lady.

PART TWO

SUMMARIES

GENERAL SUMMARY

Book One:
Boy and Girl

Dorlcote Mill, 1829. Mr and Mrs Tulliver (a Dodson before her marriage) discuss their son Tom's education. We meet Maggie, wild, clever and imaginative – her father's favourite. Her brother Tom returns from school, furious with Maggie for letting his rabbits die. Maggie suffers through Tom's punishments – she loves him so much.

Maggie embarrasses her mother in front of the respectable Dodson aunts, by cutting her hair and pushing her sweet cousin Lucy into the mud. Unhappy again because of Tom's punishments, Maggie runs away to the gypsies, but is delighted to be taken back to her beloved father.

Mr Tulliver argues with Mrs Glegg, the oldest and most difficult of his wife's sisters, who had loaned him £500. Stubbornly, Mr Tulliver decides to pay her back. He cannot afford it; he cannot demand the money that his poor sister, Mrs Moss, owes him, so he borrows from Mr Wakem, a lawyer and his enemy.

Book Two:
School-Time

Tom goes to school at Mr Stelling's and is miserable until Maggie comes to visit. Tom comes home for Christmas, but Mr Tulliver is angry about plans to take the Mill's water, and Christmas is spoilt.

Back at school, Wakem's crippled son, Philip, arrives. Tom and he are complete contrasts. They argue, partly because of their fathers' disputes. On her next visit, Maggie meets Philip and they like each other.

Time passes and Maggie, now thirteen, goes to school. Then disaster strikes and Maggie goes to fetch Tom. Their father has lost his lawsuit. He is bankrupt and dangerously ill, after suffering what is probably a heart attack.

Book Three:
The Downfall

The mortgage on the Mill is sold to Wakem. Tom, with new authority, forbids Maggie to contact Philip. The aunts arrive but they do not help and most of the Tullivers' possessions are sold.

Tom starts work for uncle Deane, vowing to pay off the family's debts. Mrs Tulliver unintentionally makes things worse when she visits Wakem, suggesting he buy the Mill and employ Tulliver. Wakem does this. Tulliver accepts the job with much bitterness, making Tom swear on the family Bible to take revenge.

Book Four:
The Valley of
Humiliation

Bob Jakin, an ex-employee, comes to the house and brings books for lonely Maggie, including *The Imitation of Christ* by Thomas à Kempis, which makes her renounce all selfish dreams. She takes up sewing to help the family.

Book Five:
Wheat and
Tares

Now seventeen, Maggie meets Philip in the Red Deeps, reminding her of the world of culture that she misses. She agrees to meet him secretly. Tom is almost ready to pay the debts when he discovers Maggie's secret. He confronts Philip insultingly.

When the debts have been paid, Tulliver attends the celebration, but on the way home he attacks Wakem, and dies the following day.

Book Six:
The Great
Temptation

Maggie, now nineteen and a governess, comes to visit her cousin Lucy, whose boyfriend, Stephen Guest, finds Maggie attractive. Philip is coming, so Maggie has to tell Lucy of their past relationship and Tom's disapproval.

Maggie asks Tom if she can meet Philip at Lucy's house. He coldly agrees. He is doing well as a partner in Guest and Co., and has persuaded uncle Deane to buy back the Mill.

Philip arrives. Lucy does not notice the feelings between Maggie and Stephen (she thinks Maggie loves Philip), but Philip is jealous because he planned to marry Maggie.

Finally, Stephen kisses Maggie. She is insulted, and goes to aunt Moss, her father's sister. Stephen follows her, and they both confess their love but they know they must part.

A boating trip is arranged for all four friends but, unfortunately, Stephen and Maggie go alone. They go so far down river that they cannot return that day. Stephen pleads with Maggie to elope with him. Next morning she refuses and sets out alone to return home.

Book Seven: The Final Rescue

Eventually, five days later, Maggie reaches St Ogg's, but Tom, now living at the Mill, disowns her. Mrs Tulliver goes with Maggie, and they call on Bob Jakin, who welcomes them. Aunt Glegg unexpectedly defends Maggie, and Philip writes her a loving letter. There is little other welcome for her: the gossips judge her behaviour cruelly, and Lucy is ill from shock. Finally, Lucy comes secretly to forgive Maggie.

Dr Kenn, the vicar and a widower, employs her, but gossip forces him to sack her. Alone on a rainy night, Maggie reads Stephen's letter, begging her to marry him. Sorely tempted, she wishes to die. The river floods. Maggie rows to the Mill to rescue Tom. Capsized by a wreck, they drown, but at last are united.

Five years later, Stephen and Philip still visit the grave in which Tom and Maggie are buried. Lucy and Stephen are married.

Detailed Summaries

Book One: Boy and Girl

Chapters 1–4: Setting the Scene

Look at the description of Maggie when she runs in – she is a problem from the beginning.

The novel opens in 1829 at Dorlcote Mill near St Ogg's on the River Floss, where a small girl is playing. Inside the Mill, Mr and Mrs Tulliver discuss their children, especially their son Tom's education and the wild cleverness of their daughter Maggie. Mr Tulliver decides to consult his friend, Mr Riley the auctioneer, about the best school for Tom.

Maggie is not considered important enough to educate – why?

Riley visits the Mill. Maggie thinks Tom is being criticised and interrupts angrily, so her father tells Riley that she is clever, which is unfortunate in a girl. Riley teases her about the book she is reading, *The History of the Devil*. Riley then recommends that Tom is sent to be educated by the Rev. Stelling, even though he really knows little about the clergyman.

Tulliver goes to fetch Tom from boarding school, without Maggie. Angrily, she goes to the attic and beats her fetish, or wooden doll, to relieve her feelings. She then goes to meets Luke, their father's miller, who tells her that Tom's rabbits, which she was supposed to look after, have died. She is upset, so Luke takes her to visit his wife.

Comment

Eliot has set the scene effectively. The Mill, which used machinery little changed for centuries, symbolises pre-industrial time. The family's parents are loving but uneducated.

Look for signs that Tulliver loves Maggie despite her mother's criticisms.

Maggie is rebellious, intelligent and full of strong feelings, e.g. her love for Tom and her anger at being laughed at or left out. She is loved by her father but her mother despairs of her wild behaviour. Her fetish represents the release of her inner passions. The dead rabbits reflect her negligence, but her fear of Tom's anger makes us sorry for her, nevertheless.

The conversation with Riley makes it clear that it is a man's world – Mrs Tulliver is foolish and was chosen for that reason by her husband, and Maggie's intelligence is criticised as unsuitable.

GLOSSARY   **withy plantation** willow trees planted by a farmer or landowner, i.e. trees that are not growing in the wild

anticipating ... sheets Mr Tulliver might have thought that Mrs Tulliver wanted him to die

mulatter half-caste

pull off my coat before I go to bed Tulliver won't give up his authority while he is alive

Manichaeism religious system founded by Manes in Persia in the 3rd century in which Satan was eternal like God

Pythoness witch

nash weak

CHAPTER 5: TOM COMES HOME

Tom's return brings joy for Maggie, but misery soon follows when he discovers about the rabbits. His anger makes her flee weeping to the attic, until their father makes Tom go to fetch her. Next morning they fish by the Round Pool and Maggie has a blissful day.

COMMENT   Maggie is very dependent on Tom's good opinion but he punishes her, just as he will later in the novel, so causing her much grief.

Notice how convincing the children's language is.   The importance of childhood experiences is mentioned on page 38: 'We could never have loved the earth so well if we had had no childhood in it'. Eliot is saying that our early lives affect our adulthood.

GLOSSARY   **phiz** face

Eagre a big wave which sometimes comes up a tidal river

Christiana Christian's wife in *Pilgrim's Progress* by John Bunyan (1628–88)

CHAPTERS 6–8: THE AUNTS AND UNCLES

The Tullivers are expecting a visit from all Mrs Tulliver's sisters and their husbands. Much food is prepared, and Tom and Maggie quarrel over a jam puff. Tom leaves her, and goes to see Bob Jakin, a boy employed to scare birds away from crops. They argue over a halfpenny which Tom believes he won.

Mrs Glegg, the eldest aunt, is the first to arrive, and she advises her sister about being economical. Mrs Pullet arrives next, in floods of ridiculous tears because an acquaintance has died. Mrs Deane arrives with Lucy.

The contrast between Maggie and Lucy is immediately established.

Maggie's untidy appearance and unbrushed hair contrasts to Lucy's neatness, as the aunts and uncles point out. Maggie goes off to cut her hair with Tom's assistance, but then is scared to come down. When she eventually comes to dinner, Mrs Tulliver and the aunts are very shocked, but Mr Tulliver comforts her.

After dinner Mr Tulliver explains his plan to send Tom to the Rev. Stelling. Mrs Glegg ridicules the idea. They quarrel, and Mrs Glegg's loan of £500 to Mr Tulliver is mentioned.

As a result, Mr Tulliver determines to pay back the loan, and visits his poor sister Mrs Moss to collect the £300 she owes him. Mr Moss says he will be ruined if he has to pay, but Tulliver remains stern until he rides away. Then he remembers that Tom is a brother to Maggie, and decides not to be hard on his sister in case Maggie suffers later. He returns to the house and says that they do not have to repay the money.

COMMENT

The Dodsons, who regard themselves as a very superior family, represent stern traditions. They are materialistic and proud, but not generous. Maggie is more like the Tulliver side of the family, and tension builds up because of these differences.

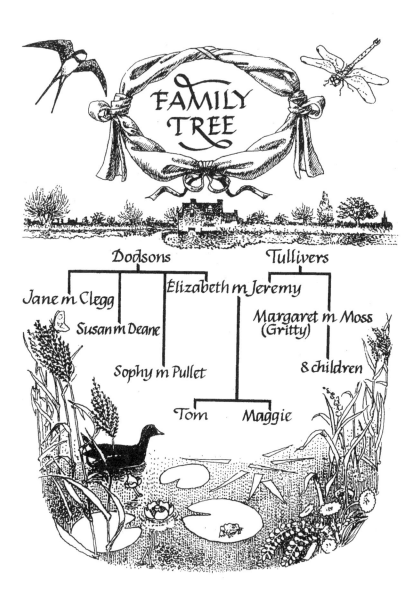

FAMILY TREE

Dodsons   Tullivers

Jane m Clegg   Elizabeth m Jeremy

    Susan m Deane   Margaret m Moss
                              (Gritty)

        Sophy m Pullet   8 children

            Tom   Maggie

Look at Tom in
these chapters: Is
he selfish?
Insensitive? Do
you like him?

The friction between Tom and Maggie shows their characters, e.g. the jam puff quarrel, Tom is unfair, Maggie is made miserable by his disapproval. The hair-cutting shows us that Maggie:

• is impetuous
• is seen as an oddity by her family
• regrets her actions

Look at how
Tulliver softens
towards his sister
and how he and
Maggie are
impetuous and
kind-hearted.

Money is an important factor in the novel. Tulliver is in debt – the road to his downfall. He does not have to pay the money, but his stubborn streak makes him determined. His visit to Mrs Moss shows poverty, in contrast to the wealthy Dodsons.

Tulliver and Aunt Moss mirror Tom and Maggie – would Tom be this kind to Maggie? Mrs Moss also seems affectionate towards Maggie, unlike the other aunts. Maggie is 'the picture of her aunt Moss' (p. 57).

GLOSSARY   **I'd as lief not invite** I would rather not invite
took her opium Maggie used her imagination to escape from her
  troubles
boluses large pills
Rhadamanthine stern and just. In classical mythology
  Rhadamanthus was a judge who decided each soul's fate
Hottentot savage
craped black cloth worn for mourning a death
Catholic Question whether Catholics should be allowed to vote
plethoric full of blood, red-faced
murrain a fatal disease in cattle

CHAPTERS 9–11: MAGGIE'S DISGRACE

After much preparation, Mrs Tulliver takes Tom, Maggie and Lucy to visit Mr and Mrs Pullet, their uncle and aunt. Maggie is in a black mood and Tom is angry with her for destroying his house of cards. Tom pays attention to Lucy – Maggie is jealous.

BOY AND GIRL

Look at how the family disapproves of Maggie.

At the Pullets' house Maggie disgraces herself by dropping her cake and spilling Tom's drink. They are sent outside to play, while Mrs Tulliver speaks to her sister about Mrs Glegg and Mr Tulliver. Suddenly, Sally the maid enters with Lucy, covered in mud.

Tom had taken Lucy to the pool to see the pike, and there Maggie pushed Lucy over. Tom had brought Lucy in, but he is also in trouble as they should not have been near the pool. He is sent to fetch Maggie, but she has disappeared. Her mother is convinced she has drowned; Tom thinks she has gone home.

Look at how imaginative Maggie is on her journey.

In fact, Maggie has run off to find the gypsies. On her way to Dunlow Common, where the gypsies camp, she meets two tramps and gives them sixpence (worth very much more then than now). Hungry and rather scared, she finds the gypsies in a lane but then she feels more

uncomfortable, as the gypsies have little food, talk strangely and steal her silver thimble. She becomes very frightened, and when a gypsy man puts her on a donkey

Their reunion confirms Tulliver's love for his 'little wench'.

to take her home, she feels as if she is in a nightmare. She is full of relief when they meet Mr Tulliver, who is so delighted that he gives the gypsy five shillings for his trouble, and insists that Maggie is not punished further.

COMMENT   Maggie continues to be in trouble over
- her appearance
- the destroyed house of cards
- the dropped cake and the spilt drink
- Lucy's fall into the mud
- her decision to run away

As in Chapter 5, she suffers because of Tom's harshness towards her. Running away to the gypsies is another example of her impetuosity (there was the hair-cutting in Chapter 7). Running away also shows that she is trying to escape from her troubled life, as well as demonstrating just how innocent she is when she is out in the wide world.

The Pullets' house, with all the keys and cupboards, symbolises the restrictive life the Dodson sisters lead. Mrs Tulliver's belief that Maggie has drowned foreshadows the book's tragic ending.

GLOSSARY   **semilunar** half-moon shape

superannuated pensioned off, old

lives too low does not spend enough

insurrectionary rebellious

Apollyon a fiend

Leonore a 'radiant maiden' in a poem by Edgar Allan Poe

CHAPTERS 12–13: THE GLEGGS AND THEIR MONEY

The legend of Ogg the ferryman is told. Many years before, he had transported travellers across the river, and one stormy night a mother and child wanted to cross. When they arrived on the far bank, the woman became the Virgin Mary and blessed Ogg.

Maggie is linked to the river and the Virgin of St Ogg's later in the book.

Mr and Mrs Glegg live in St Ogg's, a town with a long history. At breakfast, soon after the argument with Tulliver, Mrs Glegg picks a quarrel with her husband because she thinks he disagrees about recalling

the debt. Finally she decides not to ask for the money –
yet.

Mrs Pullet finds it easy to plead Mrs Tulliver's case the
next day as Mrs Glegg says she will not demand the
money. However, Tulliver, angered by his wife's plan,
has already written to say that he will pay the £500 by
next month. He is forced to borrow the money from a
man he dislikes, the lawyer Wakem.

COMMENT   The St Ogg legend is important because:
- it creates a sense of history for the town
- it reminds us of the river **motif** (see Literary Terms)
  so important later in the book, and symbolises time
  passing
- it symbolises Maggie – the Virgin of St Ogg's

There is humour in the way in which the Glegg's
marriage is described: Eliot's use of **satire** (see Literary
Terms) and humour to poke fun at the characters
lightens the mood of the novel.

Money, particularly the themes of debt and wealth, is
still an important factor. Tulliver's stubborn decision to
borrow the £500 to repay the debt begins a sequence of
events which leads to his ruin.

GLOSSARY   **unlade** unload
              hagiographer someone who writes about the lives of saints
              praeterite past
              weeper long black ribbons used to show mourning
              Oedipus figure from Greek mythology who had a tragic life

Identify the speaker.

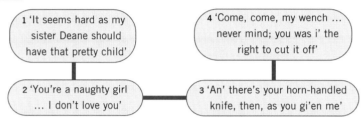

1 'It seems hard as my sister Deane should have that pretty child'

4 'Come, come, my wench ... never mind; you was i' the right to cut it off'

2 'You're a naughty girl ... I don't love you'

3 'An' there's your horn-handled knife, then, as you gi'en me'

Identify the person 'to whom' this comment refers.

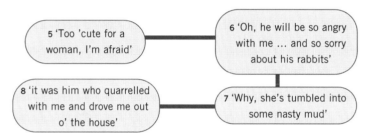

5 'Too 'cute for a woman, I'm afraid'

6 'Oh, he will be so angry with me ... and so sorry about his rabbits'

8 'it was him who quarrelled with me and drove me out o' the house'

7 'Why, she's tumbled into some nasty mud'

Check your answers on page 84.

 Consider these issues.

a The contrast between Maggie and Lucy: think about the qualities required to be an ideal Victorian girl. Why does Maggie's behaviour create problems?

b What we learn about the family differences between the Dodson sisters and the Tullivers – your thoughts about Maggie's aunts and their treatment of her.

c How the historical and descriptive details of the town, and the legend of St Ogg's make the setting real for us.

d The **symbolism** (see Literary Terms) of any mention of rivers, floods and drowning which prepare us for the later action.

e Why Eliot considers childhood important: look at Maggie/Tom and Tulliver/Mrs Moss.

f How Eliot uses the 'inner voice' of a character to let us know what they are really thinking, and the dialect in speech to make it realistic.

BOOK TWO: SCHOOL-TIME

CHAPTER 1: TOM'S 'FIRST HALF'

Tom's education at Mr Stelling's is rather severe and lonely. Desperately shy, he can barely ask for more pudding, and he studies difficult subjects. Mr Stelling, a greedy and ambitious man who wants more pupils, hopes to impress with Tom's progress in a classical education. He has neither interest in nor understanding of what Tulliver wants for Tom, or what suits the boy. Tom also has to look after the Stellings' daughter, Laura, after the birth of their second child.

Notice Maggie's Tom is pleased when Maggie is brought to stay,
need for approval although her natural quickness and liking for his
and admiration. detested lessons annoy him. He is delighted when Mr Stelling dismisses her as 'shallow'.

COMMENT Although in Book One we might have thought Tom was too hard on Maggie, this episode makes us like him
Tom becomes more now that he, too, is suffering. He:
'more like a girl' • suffers, Stelling does not teach him anything
(p. 141) because of appropriate or enjoyable
his experience. • is treated as stupid and laughed at
• is lonely, and appreciates Maggie when she visits
• seems less arrogant and cocksure
• is kind to Stelling's small daughter, Laura

Maggie's visit is important in establishing some important aspects of her character. She enjoys being admired by Mr Stelling (p. 151), but she is easily deflated by his remarks about the shallow nature of female intelligence. This scene shows how very dependent Maggie is on the approval of others.

A minor theme in the book is Eliot's criticism of this kind of classical education. Notice her use of **satire** (see Literary Terms) to describe vain, shallow Mr Stelling.

'My name is Norval' a passage from *Douglas*, a play by John
Home (1724–1808) often given to pupils to recite
percussion-caps small explosive devices, to be used in a toy
revolver
peccavi (Latin) I have sinned

CHAPTER 2: THE CHRISTMAS HOLIDAYS

Tom returns home to a beautiful Christmas scene, but
Mr Tulliver is quarrelsome because a neighbour is
trying to divert part of the River Ripple (a tributary of
the Floss) to irrigate his land. He feels Wakem is

See how, as in   responsible. The Moss family are at the house, and his
Book One, his   wife and his sister try to persuade him not to go to law.
wife's influence
fails to change   The Tullivers learn that Philip, Wakem's son and a
Tulliver's mind.   cripple, will go to Mr Stelling too. Tulliver is rather
flattered that both boys will enjoy the same advantage.
Tom is not so sure.

COMMENT   Look at the skilful way in which Eliot creates a perfect
Eliot portrays the   Christmas scene, then shows how Tulliver's
children's worries   argumentative, stubborn streak spoils it for the children.
very well.   This builds **narrative tension** (see Literary Terms).

GLOSSARY   *a priori* **ground** (Latin) meaning 'from the former', because Moss
feels obliged to support Tulliver because he is family and has
lent him money

CHAPTERS 3 AND 4: TOM AND PHILIP

Note the   Reluctantly, Tom returns to Mr Stelling's, and meets
contrasting   Philip who is very shy and self-conscious. Tom dislikes
descriptions of the   Philip for being Wakem's son, and because he has a
boys.   humpback, but he is impressed by how well he draws
and his ability to tell exciting stories.

Tom is confused as to how Wakem could have a
likeable son, and Philip politely tries not to laugh at

Notice how the boys are as distant and different as their fathers.

Tom's silly comments. Philip helps Tom with his Latin and tells him stories, but Tom's occasional insensitive comments make Philip moody. Philip is soon offended by Tom's thoughtless reference to his physical weakness, and Tom is insulted by Philip's comments about fishing. Typically, Tom is unaware of what he has done wrong, and thinks Philip's mood are confirmation that all hunchbacks are disagreeable.

The boys' education is described, and it is clear that Mr Stelling is a poor teacher. Tom suffers less, however, now Philip is there. Mr Poulter, the village schoolmaster and an old soldier, helps Tom by telling him war stories. Tom tries to get Philip to watch Mr Poulter's sword exercise, but the idea of physical skill makes Philip bitter about his own weaknesses so they argue. Tom calls Lawyer Wakem a rogue, offending Philip. Mr Poulter lends Tom his sword.

COMMENT

Eliot's criticism of education continues, she sees it as 'entirely a matter of luck'. Look at the **irony** (see Literary Terms) of the way Stelling's system suits Philip but not Tom, but Tom benefits from Mr Poulter's unconventional methods.

Their uneasy friendship strengthens the sense of tension in this section.

We are also shown the extreme difference between the sensitive character of the deformed Philip, and the inflexible, unfeeling character of Tom in Chapter 3 when they meet. Eliot makes the speech of the boys very realistic and uses their 'inner voices' (see Language and Style) to reveal the differences in each boy's approach to life.

GLOSSARY

Propia quae maribus (Latin) meaning 'matters pertaining to the sea'. From the Latin grammar Tom had to learn
not a congenital hump Philip has had an accident, he was not born with a hump
superannuated charger an old war horse

Semele a girl in Greek mythology, loved by Jupiter and killed by the sight of him as a thunderbolt

Arne an English composer

Bony Napoleon Bonaparte

CHAPTERS 5 AND 6: MAGGIE VISITS TOM

Maggie's eyes are also admired by her father - they reflect her intelligence.

Tom cannot understand why Philip remains angry at his insulting remark about his father. Maggie arrives, fascinated by the clever, deformed son of their father's enemy, and Philip, interested by Maggie's dark eyes, thinks her a nice little thing. Tom takes Maggie up to see the sword, and while he is swinging it he cuts his foot badly and faints.

Tom is worried that he may be left crippled by the injury, but is too frightened to ask anyone. Sensitive to Tom's fears, Philip asks Mr Stelling himself, and is able to reassure Tom that he will recover completely. Tom is full of joy and gratitude, and for a while the boys are friends again.

Note the similarities between Maggie and Philip.

Maggie talks warmly to Philip, kisses him in an innocent way and promises to be like a sister to him. After she leaves, the boys go back to their uneasy friendship.

COMMENT   Maggie's visits are important since they both maintain a link with the principal character and allow further development of her character, showing her:

- intelligence and enthusiasm
- need for love and approval
- love and sensitivity
- bond to her family

An important link is made between Maggie and Philip Wakem in their childhood years. Philip shows an immediate affection for her (p. 179) and Maggie's promise to kiss him next time they meet shows her understanding that Philip needs love, just as she does.

The conflict between the boys echoes that between

their fathers: the tension is increased by Maggie's simple liking for Philip, which prepares us for later developments in the plot.

GLOSSARY   **wry-necked** with a twisted neck

Philoctetes in Greek mythology he was one of Jason's Argonauts who had a wounded foot, but was miraculously healed

the grey colt ...black sire Philip may look like his mother, but might behave as badly as his father

CHAPTER 7: THE GOLDEN GATES ARE PASSED

Tom is now sixteen and still with Mr Stelling, and although the work is no less boring, he has matured. Thirteen-year-old Maggie is at boarding school and is now quite the young lady. She rarely sees Philip and, when she does, knows that her childish promise to kiss him is now 'out of the question' (p. 187). Tulliver's lawsuit continues, with Wakem acting against him, and Tom's friendship with Philip has cooled.

Notice how Tom reacts to the bad news compared to Maggie. One November evening, Maggie arrives unexpectedly at Mr Stelling's and tells Tom that their father has lost his lawsuit and the family has lost everything. Mr Tulliver is also gravely ill. Brother and sister go home.

COMMENT   This is a **climactic** (see Literary Terms) chapter, where the tensions about money and the lawsuit come to a head. Eliot makes it clear that the 'golden gates' of childhood are now closed behind Tom and Maggie as their poverty and suffering begin.

It is **ironic** (see Literary Terms) that the brother and sister are united as they leave the Stellings': their different reactions reflect the conflict brewing between them. Tom thinks of his lost inheritance and the shame – his face is 'rigid and tearless' (p. 192), while Maggie is concerned for her father and weeps emotionally.

GLOSSARY   **accoutrements** equipment

virgin razor unused: he was too young to need to use his razor

A Identify the speaker.

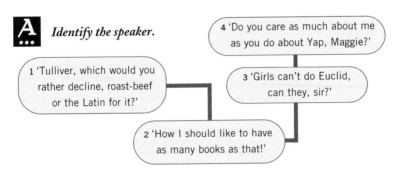

1 'Tulliver, which would you rather decline, roast-beef or the Latin for it?'

2 'How I should like to have as many books as that!'

3 'Girls can't do Euclid, can they, sir?'

4 'Do you care as much about me as you do about Yap, Maggie?'

Identify the person 'to whom' this comment refers.

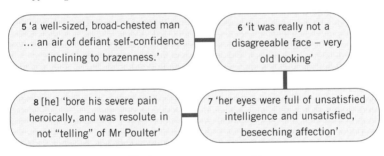

5 'a well-sized, broad-chested man ... an air of defiant self-confidence inclining to brazenness.'

6 'it was really not a disagreeable face – very old looking'

7 'her eyes were full of unsatisfied intelligence and unsatisfied, beseeching affection'

8 [he] 'bore his severe pain heroically, and was resolute in not "telling" of Mr Poulter'

Check your answers on page 84.

B Consider these issues.

a The ways in which Tom is hard towards Maggie and insensitive to Philip: how Eliot makes sure that we do not dislike him despite these faults, and how Tom becomes 'more like a girl'.

b How different aspects of Maggie's character are shown.

c The similarities between Maggie and Philip, and the contrast between Philip and Tom. How Philip is not a typical boy, nor Maggie a typical girl.

d The importance of money and the sense of doom once the lawsuit is lost.

e What Eliot makes us feel about the Stellings and conventional education.

f Eliot's descriptive and dramatic writing: look at Christmas (Chapter 2) and the accident with the sword (Chapter 5).

BOOK THREE: THE DOWNFALL

CHAPTERS 1 AND 2: COMING HOME

Characteristically, Tulliver stubbornly refuses to see the seriousness of the situation.   The details of Tulliver's bankruptcy are given: at first he believes he will be able to continue at the Mill as a tenant. Further money problems are mentioned – he had to pay out £250 when his friend Riley died, and the man who lent him the £500 to pay Mrs Glegg demanded the furniture as surety if Tulliver did not pay his debt.

Tulliver writes to Maggie, asking her to come home from school. His lawyer, Mr Gore, had left a letter at his office for Tulliver, and on his way home Tulliver stops his horse to read it: the mortgage on the Mill has been transferred to his enemy, Wakem. He falls in shock to the ground where he is found by his waggoner.

Tulliver still shows affection for Maggie.   Maggie comes home to find her father barely conscious, asking for his 'little wench'.

The aunts arrive. Maggie remains by her father's bedside until she goes alone to fetch Tom, against her aunts' advice. In the coach, on the way back to the Mill, Tom forbids Maggie to speak to Philip again.

The children's different reactions to the troubles reflect their personalities.   When they arrive home, the bailiff is in the house, which shocks Tom. They find their mother in her storeroom looking at her precious china and linen. She is more concerned about losing them than about her husband whom she blames for their plight. Tom seems to agree with her, and Maggie is angry with them both for being so unfeeling. After seeing his father, however, Tom is affected by grief and he and Maggie are united once more.

COMMENT   Tulliver's downfall is described in detail. Eliot shows his character, stubborn to the last, in this 'puzzling world' (p. 198). She shows how even unimportant people 'have their tragedy too' (p. 199), reflecting her intention of portraying the pain in humble lives.

The plot, which has built up tension concerning the lawsuit, culminates as Tulliver is placed in Wakem's power. The importance of money and the terror of poverty is shown again.

Note how it was always her father who had defended her previously.

The different reactions reflect the family's contrasts and divisions. Mrs Tulliver's trivial mourning for the fate of her linen and Tom's new indignation against his father contrast with Maggie's strong love and defence of Tulliver.

Tom's character is hardening and he has new authority in the family:
- he tells Maggie not to see Philip
- he plans to get a 'situation' to earn money
- he knows he must take care of his mother
- he feels anger at his father's behaviour

GLOSSARY   **teraphim** an idol or image of a god

chany china

egoistic resentment personal anger; here Maggie's anger against her mother

CHAPTERS 3–5: THE AUNTS AND UNCLES

Although aunt Deane is wealthy enough to help the Tullivers, it is obvious that the Dodson aunts will only give gloomy advice. Mrs Tulliver wants to sell them her best things, but they will not buy, and Mrs Glegg is annoyed by Tom's practical suggestion to give him and Maggie their inheritance now. They criticise Tulliver, and Maggie bursts out that they are not helping, but interfering. Aunt Moss arrives, very upset, wishing that she could pay back Tulliver's £300, but Tom insists that his father wishes to destroy the note promising payment. They go to Tulliver's room to find it.

Maggie's defiant speaking of the truth contrasts with Tom's mature restraint.

Tom's behaviour makes him seem mature and likeable at this point.

While looking for the note, the lid of the chest falls with a crash, waking Tulliver. He remembers most of his troubles, including owing Luke £50, and he shows anger against Wakem, telling Tom to punish him, before becoming unconscious again. Tom then destroys the note, and vows to pay Luke, even out of his and Maggie's savings.

Note how Eliot uses humour to criticise this kind of education.

Next day, Tom goes to St Ogg's to ask his uncle Deane to find him employment. It becomes clear that uncle Deane despises classical education, and although Tom promises that he will soon forget all he knows, he realises that he will have to learn book-keeping. On his way home, he sees a bill announcing the sale of Dorlcote Mill, and arrives home in a bad temper, which he takes out on Maggie, scolding her for being rude to the aunts. Maggie is once again heart-broken at his stern words.

C OMMENT

Note how her impetuous nature recalls her father's behaviour.

The contrast between the wealthy Dodson aunts, who could afford to help the Tullivers, and poor aunt Moss, who would if she could, shows the lack of generosity in the Dodson side of the family, and we feel Maggie's criticism of them is brave and justified, even if rather foolish.

Tom is maturing, showing several good points. He:

- is sensible during the discussion with the aunts
- is honourable in his decision not to make the Moss's sell up to repay their debt
- wants to honour the debt to Luke with his own and Maggie's money
- is determined to get a job

He is, however, hard on Maggie when she needs love, he understands the meanness of the aunts and he is critical of their father.

Mrs Tulliver's foolish obsession with her china creates divisions between her and Maggie and it is clear that they are increasingly distant from each other.

GLOSSARY   **Homer** ancient Greek poet, believed to have written the *Iliad* and the *Odyssey*

sanative healthful

prosy dull

Dominie Sampson schoolmaster in *Guy Mannering*, a novel by Sir Walter Scott (1771–1832)

CHAPTERS 6–9: DEALING WITH DISGRACE

In December, the Tullivers' furniture is sold, and the family sit in their father's room, worried that he might wake up and realise what is happening. After the sale, a man arrives, wanting to see Tom. It is Bob Jakin, to whom he gave a pocket-knife when they were children. Maggie bursts in, full of grief that their childhood books had been sold along with almost everything else. For friendship, Bob tries to give Tom nine sovereigns even though it is all he has. He plans to travel, selling goods from a pack. Tom and Maggie are touched, but graciously refuse the gift.

Tulliver slowly recovers physically, but his problems worsen. The land, stock and the Mill are to be sold,

Eliot continues to mock the lack of generosity of the family.

and although Guest and Co. might buy the Mill and leave Tulliver as manager, they are afraid that Wakem might decide to bid. The family will not help financially, but Mr Glegg will take Mrs Tulliver a pound of tea (tea was an expensive luxury at the time). Mr Deane, however, finds a warehouse job for Tom.

Once again, Mrs Tulliver's efforts have the opposite effect to what she intended.

Mrs Tulliver goes to see Wakem, to beg him not to bid for the estate. He had not intended to do so, but when he realises that Guest and Co. are interested he quickly decides to buy it. He has been insulted by Tulliver and is pleased to humiliate him.

A January day, and Tulliver finally goes downstairs, unaware of who has bought the Mill. The aunts think that Tulliver ought to be grateful to Wakem for a chance to earn a living. Maggie is worried about his reaction to the news. As Tulliver is looking through the dates in the family Bible, his wife mentions that Wakem now owns the Mill, and wants to employ him.

Maggie is sensitive to her father's feelings.

After several days of struggle, Tulliver decides to accept Wakem's offer of a job. It is mainly his love for his boyhood home that persuades him to stay, and his promise to his wife. That night, a bitter Tulliver orders Tom to write a curse in the family Bible and demands that he have revenge on Wakem if he can.

COMMENT

Note the contrast between the cold Dodson aunts and Bob's warmth. It is clear that Eliot judges a character by his actions rather than his class. Bob Jakin's simple country speech shows him to be a humble character, but he is prepared to give nearly all of his money to help a friend, as would poor aunt Moss.

The lowest point is reached: Tulliver faces the final humiliation of having to work for his enemy. The importance of money and the threat of poverty is now a reality.

Mrs Tulliver's   There is some black humour in this section as Mrs
insensitivity   Tulliver unwittingly reminds Wakem of her healthy son
matches her son's.   and his crippled one.

The importance of childhood is mentioned, with
Tulliver's decision to take the job because of his
memories based at the Mill, his boyhood home; and the
mention of Bob and Tom's shared childhood.

The theme of revenge with the **allusion** (see Literary
Terms) to curses, the devil and the use of the Bible,
brings this section to a dark close, building tension and
hinting at the threat of further conflict. The family's
burden is willingly shouldered by Tom.

GLOSSARY   **pigs' chitterlings** edible entrails of a pig

suffer a waste of tissue by evaporation lose weight through
sweating

transported criminal punishment, to be sent out of the country
perhaps to Australia

eidolon phantom

Yellow candidate a person trying to be elected to the House of
Commons

sangfroid coolness in difficult circumstances

chiaroscuro contrasting, taken from painting using light and
shade

Saturnalian exciting, wild, from the ancient Roman festival of
Saturnalia

rust on the wheat a mould which kills the crop

Identify the speaker.

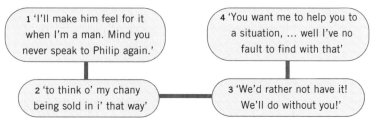

1 'I'll make him feel for it when I'm a man. Mind you never speak to Philip again.'

4 'You want me to help you to a situation, ... well I've no fault to find with that'

2 'to think o' my chany being sold in i' that way'

3 'We'd rather not have it! We'll do without you!'

Identify the person 'to whom' this comment refers.

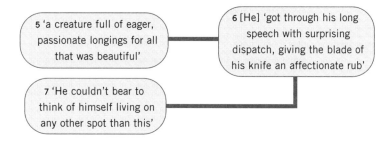

5 'a creature full of eager, passionate longings for all that was beautiful'

6 [He] 'got through his long speech with surprising dispatch, giving the blade of his knife an affectionate rub'

7 'He couldn't bear to think of himself living on any other spot than this'

Check your answers on page 84.

 Consider these issues.

a The aunts' response to the Tullivers' distress, Bob's response and the response of aunt Moss. Think about Eliot's message here and of whom she approves.

b Tom is maturing – do you like him better? What do you think of his behaviour to Maggie? To aunt Moss? To Bob? His reaction to the news of the bankruptcy?

c The revenge theme – what significance it has on the plot.

d Tom's and Maggie's differences: a clash seems inevitable.

e How Eliot brings the Tulliver family to the lowest point in their fortunes. List the problems they face.

f Tulliver's isolation physically and socially: the narrative tension (see Literary Terms) because he is only half-aware of events.

BOOKS FOUR AND FIVE: HUMILIATION AND WHEAT AND TARES

BOOK FOUR: CHAPTER 1: A VARIATION OF PROTESTANTISM

Eliot was one of the first novelists to focus on the lives of such humble folk.

The chapter uses an **authorial voice** (see Literary Terms), describing the dreary castles on the River Rhône, and apologising for the narrow, oppressive atmosphere of the story. She says we need to understand what life was like for Tom and Maggie to appreciate its effect. The similarities and differences between the Tulliver and Dodson families are shown.

COMMENT

The story's narrative flow is interrupted as Eliot provides insight into the lives of the two principal families: the stern nature of the Dodsons and the 'generous imprudence' of the Tullivers. The **allusion** (see Literary Terms) to religion, and the way that the families seem to have no real Christian beliefs fits well with the selfishness of the aunts and Tulliver's vindictive curse.

The **theme** (see Literary Terms) of the tragedy of humble people is continued through Tom's and Maggie's sufferings.

The river **motif** (see Literary Terms) reappears in references to the flood (p. 276) and 'the great old river' (p. 276).

GLOSSARY

The Valley of Humiliation from John Bunyan's *Pilgrim's Progress*

Bossuet French bishop (1627–1704) renowned for his preaching and defence of Roman Catholicism against Protestantism

fromenty a drink made from whole wheat boiled in milk and sweetened with sugar and spice; also called frumenty

BOOK FOUR: CHAPTERS 2 AND 3: MISERY AND RENUNCIATION

Maggie's life sinks into dull monotony and loneliness. Tom is obsessed with working; Mrs Tulliver is bewildered, but nevertheless does the hardest of the housework to save Maggie's hands; Mr Tulliver is silent and depressed, only concerned with repaying his creditors. He thinks about Maggie, and how unlikely it is that she will marry well.

One miserable day in spring, Maggie is seated sadly outside when a man with a pack arrives. Bob Jakin brings Maggie a parcel of books as a present and they talk in a friendly manner.

Maggie's conversion is sympathetically drawn – Eliot had a similar experience at this age. One of the books Bob has brought is *The Imitation of Christ* by Thomas à Kempis, which teaches the renunciation of self-love. After reading it Maggie decides to help the family by earning money through sewing. It is **ironic** (see Literary Terms) that this causes conflict with Tom, whose pride makes him dislike his sister asking for work. It makes her father still more sad that she will be wasted in a poor marriage, while her mother is pleased, but puzzled that she is 'growing up so good' (p. 299).

COMMENT The misery of the whole family is shown and they seem lonely and distant from each other.

Maggie's character is developing, although she still lacks self-command (p. 280). She renounces all her dreams, but it is a sad existence and her efforts do not bring happiness to her father or brother, the people she loves best.

The recurring **theme** (see Literary Terms) of Bob's generosity and his admiration for Maggie is a ray of sunshine in a miserable time, he sees her as a 'directing Madonna' (p. 290), and Eliot's **allusion** (see Literary Terms) to knights (p. 290) makes Bob almost a heroic figure.

GLOSSARY   **incubus** nightmare, the demon who appears to sleepers

sawney fool

Burke Edmund Burke, a political thinker and speaker (1729–97)

say-so small amount of money

BOOK FIVE: CHAPTERS 1 AND 2: MAGGIE'S AND TOM'S SUFFERING

In June, Maggie sees Philip ride into the mill-yard with his father, but she makes herself ignore him, despite remembering the childish affection she once had for him. She walks through the Red Deeps, her favourite haunt. Philip meets her there – he is in love with her: he carries the picture of her he drew five years earlier.

The importance of Maggie does not return these feelings: she is reminded *childhood* of her childhood friendship and feels sorry for Philip; *memories is* and she agrees to meet him again, even though an inner *conveyed here.* voice warns her that it is wrong.

Tom is working hard and Mr Deane is impressed by his head for business, but making money is a slow business. Bob Jakin suggests that Tom joins him in a small business venture: buying goods to sell abroad. Tom agrees, but has to ask his father for the money. Tulliver is unwilling to part with any money in case it is lost, so Tom goes to see Mr Glegg instead, taking Bob along to relieve the embarrassment. An amusing scene follows, during which Mrs Glegg buys some of Bob's goods and agrees to lend Tom the 'nest-egg'. By the time Maggie meets Philip, Tom has made nearly £150 – a very substantial sum in the early nineteenth century.

COMMENT   'Wheat and Tares', the title of this section, has biblical **allusions** (see Literary Terms) and reflects its mixture of sadness and happiness.

The two chapters show the contrasting experiences of Maggie and Tom.

Although both are unhappy:
- Tom's character is very different from Maggie's – he is resolved and single-minded, she wavers and agrees to meet Philip
- as a man, Tom is able to take an active role, working and earning money, unlike Maggie who cannot really help economically and is forced into a passive role
- Tom has some success to celebrate through making money
- Tom can go out and meet people, e.g. Bob and Mr Glegg, unlike lonely Maggie who must be secretive
- the humour in Tom's chapter contrasts with the **pathos** (see Literary Terms) in Maggie's
- Maggie is concerned about Tom and her father, for Tom dislikes being at home

Notice Eliot's poetic description of the wood. The beauty of the Red Deeps is **symbolic** (see Literary Terms) as is its name, with the bluebells like a glimpse of heaven contrasting with the ugliness of Maggie's life. It is 'deep' and shadowy, reflecting the secret meetings with Philip that will take place there.

Maggie's deprivation is shown: her soul hungers for the world of books, music and art that Philip represents. There will be problems ahead for Maggie, as she seems full of conflicting forces (p. 305).

Maggie is now beautiful, but her innocence and naivety is conveyed by her child-like greeting to Philip (p. 306) and her unawareness that he could be her suitor (p. 310). Eliot suggests that Philip is wrong to suggest they meet, although his motives are good (p. 314).

Eliot reminds us of the river motif: a hint of the book's ending. Maggie's love for Tom, and the childhood memories of him, are shown: her first memory is 'standing with Tom by the side of the Floss, while he held my hand' (p. 313), and this reminds us of the possible danger created by the meeting.

Note Mr Glegg's
surprise that Bob
will not take any
of Tom's profits.

The encounter between Bob and Mrs Glegg is amusing, but it has its serious side, reflecting Bob's warm nature and his business sense – he persuades the Gleggs to invest in Tom's enterprise. Bob's generosity helps Tom get closer to his dream of repaying the debts.

GLOSSARY   tares weeds

avaunt go away

Hecuba in Greek mythology the wife of Priam, King of Troy

Aaron Moses' brother

bathos a serious point followed by an ordinary one, anti-climax

BOOK FIVE: CHAPTERS 3–5: LOVE DISCOVERED

Maggie is tempted to meet Philip, but she is determined not to see him again. Philip warns her that her renunciation is 'stupefying' her, and she needs the books and art that he can bring her: he shows her *Maggie's feelings* kindness and Maggie almost wishes he could have been *for Philip are* her brother. Finally Philip says that he will walk in the *sisterly, not* woods and so meet her accidentally. Maggie's resolve is *passionate.* broken, she agrees to meet him.

Nearly a year later we see the couple at one of their secret meetings, exchanging books happily. Maggie complains that the heroines in novels are always blond, *Philip's prediction* and Philip jokes that Maggie will one day take love *will prove true.* from her blond cousin Lucy. Philip confesses his feelings for Maggie; she is surprised and worried. It is clear that her feelings do not mirror his, but she kisses him and wants to make him happy.

Maggie dreads Tom or her father discovering her secret. The next Sunday, aunt Pullet visits the Tulliver's and mentions that she has seen Philip coming out of the Red Deeps several times. Tom notices Maggie's blush at these words and guesses her secret. Furiously he confronts Maggie, telling her that he will come with her to meet Philip and forcing her to swear on the

There is a dim sense of relief, as Maggie has realised she does not really love Philip.

Bible that she will not see Philip again, or else he will tell their father. Maggie, not wanting to hurt her father, swears. She is pleased that the debts will soon be paid, but Tom makes her feel guilty.

When Tom meets Philip he treats him with contempt and insults his crippled body. Maggie is horrified and tells Tom that he has no pity, and has always enjoyed punishing her. Maggie goes home in tears.

COMMENT

Maggie and Philip are both outsiders and different from the 'norm' of their day.

Philip and Maggie share a common fate: Philip is described as 'queer and lonely' (p. 346) and Maggie is an isolated figure. It is understandable that they should be drawn together. Maggie's motives are pure, she is shown to be like a child with Philip and is genuinely surprised at his declaration of love (p. 341), and Philip's feminine nature (p. 344) ensures there is no sexual attraction on Maggie's part. Although the meetings are socially wrong and against the family's wishes, we sympathise with them as they have suffered, especially after Tom's cruel attack on Philip.

The Bible recalls Tulliver's curse and Tom's promise to have revenge.

The fear that the doomed relationship will be discovered gives this section a **narrative tension** (see Literary Terms) that builds up from the swearing on the Bible to reach its climax as Tom confronts Philip.

At the end of this section, Tom and Maggie are more distant than ever before. There is a similarity to the pattern of their childhood which Maggie mentions (p. 354).

BOOK FIVE: CHAPTERS 6 AND 7: TRIUMPH AND DISASTER

Three weeks later Tom comes home and asks his father to count the money – he has enough in the bank to pay the debts and he has organised a dinner for the creditors. Tulliver is delighted that Wakem will know of the news and rejoices in his pride that his son is not

Note the similar attitudes of father and son.

crippled. He tells Tom to try to buy back the Mill.
Maggie is delighted by the news, even though Tom is
cold to her.

Ironically,
Tulliver is
unaware how
Tom's education
hindered him.

Tulliver is his old self again, and at the dinner he makes
a speech, explaining his pride in what Tom has done.
Tom makes a speech too, and Tulliver tells his friends
that he gave Tom an expensive education. The party
breaks up and Tulliver sets off for home. When he
arrives at the Mill he meets Wakem and attacks him.
Maggie comes to Wakem's rescue, but then Tulliver
collapses. When Tom returns with Bob, he is annoyed
that his triumphant day has been spoilt by another's
wrong-doing. During the night, Tulliver's condition
gets worse and he dies at dawn. Tom and Maggie are
united once more in their grief.

COMMENT
Tom's cold cruelty to Maggie and Philip means that
the reader does not completely share his sense of
triumph when the debts are paid, and Tulliver's
reaction – to think of continuing his vendetta with
Wakem is a continuation of the revenge **motif** (see
Literary Terms).

Their father's seizure after the stupid brawl gives
another opportunity to show Tom's and Maggie's

Humiliation and wheat and tares

They were united contrasting reactions to events: Tom is 'dejected' that
after the lawsuit his triumph has been spoilt, Maggie keeps reliving 'the
was lost at the end agony of the moment' (p. 365). However they are
of Book Two. united, even though it seems that they need supreme
suffering to bring them together.

Notice that for The helpless situation of women in Victorian society is
much of Books clearly brought out. Maggie's dependence is
Four and Five emphasised: unable to contribute to the finances of the
Maggie is isolated family, she has no part in Tom's triumph, and she has
and helpless. to obey him about Philip.

TEST YOURSELF (BOOKS FOUR AND FIVE)

A *Identify the speaker.*

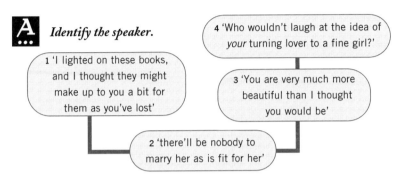

4 'Who wouldn't laugh at the idea of *your* turning lover to a fine girl?'

1 'I lighted on these books, and I thought they might make up to you a bit for them as you've lost'

3 'You are very much more beautiful than I thought you would be'

2 'there'll be nobody to marry her as is fit for her'

Identify the person 'to whom' this comment refers.

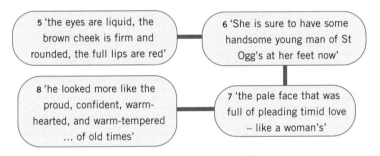

5 'the eyes are liquid, the brown cheek is firm and rounded, the full lips are red'

6 'She is sure to have some handsome young man of St Ogg's at her feet now'

8 'he looked more like the proud, confident, warm-hearted, and warm-tempered ... of old times'

7 'the pale face that was full of pleading timid love – like a woman's'

Check your answers on page 84.

B *Consider these issues.*

a References to the flood motif: look how Eliot weaves it into this section to keep it in our minds.

b Maggie's conversion: how Eliot makes a sympathetic and realistic picture of her suffering and attempts to cope, and the dramatic change in Maggie which results in inner turmoil.

c The importance of money and the need to pay creditors. Tom is able to take action, but look at Maggie's role and her isolation in the family.

d The mixture of happiness and tragedy: in Maggie's relationship with Philip, Tulliver's triumph and death, Eliot is making a realistic picture of life. Is she successful?

e The conflict between Tom and Maggie, and Tom's cruelty to Philip – look how it follows the pattern established in childhood.

f Maggie's innocence: how Eliot keeps Maggie's motives pure in her relationship with Philip and why.

BOOKS SIX AND SEVEN: TEMPTATION AND RESCUE

BOOK SIX: CHAPTERS 1–3: MEETING STEPHEN GUEST

Two years have passed and Lucy is at her father's house with Stephen Guest, her boyfriend. Lucy is still in mourning for her mother, who had died some time before, and Mrs Tulliver is now their housekeeper. Maggie, who has become a teacher, is expected to visit soon. Lucy plays a joke on Stephen, allowing him to believe that Maggie is like her mother.

Lucy is kind and generous in her plans for Maggie's happiness.

When she arrives Maggie is emotional at being back in St Ogg's, and at the mention of Philip's name, so that when Stephen enters and shows his surprise at her appearance, she is unable to make simple polite conversation, and is rather outspoken. Maggie listens attentively as Stephen talks about a book he had read, and Lucy is pleased they like each other. They go to the river and Stephen is aware that he is interested in Maggie, and Maggie enjoys his attentions. On their return, aunt Pullet, shocked by Maggie's poor clothes, tries to find an evening dress for her.

Stephen is instantly attracted to Maggie who, unused to society, is unconsciously flattered by him.

That night, alone, Maggie is thinking of her delight at being in a world of love and pleasure when Lucy comes to her room. When Philip's planned visit is mentioned, Maggie explains that she cannot see him because of her promise to Tom, and then she tells her of the love affair, and how the families would never consent. Lucy thinks it is beautiful that Maggie should love Philip.

Lucy's belief that Maggie loves Philip makes her blind to Maggie's and Stephen's growing attraction.

COMMENT First impressions of Stephen are not good: he is 'drowsy' when Tom's hard work is mentioned (p. 375) suggesting lazy indifference, he treats Lucy like a child and has chosen her because she is a 'little darling' (p. 379) rather than an equal. (There is an echo here of Mr Tulliver's remarks about the reasons why he chose his wife (p. 16).) There is no meeting of minds with

The lightness of Lucy's and Stephen's lives contrast with the drudgery of Maggie's and Tom's.

Lucy, in contrast to Maggie, who is intelligent and challenging (p. 385).

Lucy's goodness is emphasised through her plans for Maggie's and Mrs Tulliver's enjoyment. It is made clear that she is unaware of Maggie's and Stephen's attraction.

Maggie is uncomfortable when Philip's name is mentioned.

Maggie's confession to Lucy is 'blinding' (p. 397) because she does not fully explain that her feelings for Philip are sisterly, not passionate. Lucy makes her own romantic story about the relationship, not noticing Maggie and Stephen are falling in love.

GLOSSARY

attar of roses perfume

da capo from the beginning (Italian)

Raphael an archangel

merino soft woollen fabric

downy-lipped alumnus young student (who does not yet need to shave)

Sir Andrew Aguecheek a foolish character in Shakespeare's *Twelfth Night*

BOOK SIX: CHAPTERS 4 AND 5: TOM AND MAGGIE

The conversation between Maggie and Tom is similar to when they were children.

Maggie visits Tom, who is lodging with Bob Jakin in his rather poor house by the river. Tom's first words are cold and hard as Maggie asks if she might see Philip again at Lucy's house. Tom says that she may, although he has no faith in her inconsistent nature. Nevertheless they part on a warm note.

Tom visits uncle Deane, who commends his hard work and tells him that he will get a share in the business. Tom asks if the firm would try to buy Dorlcote Mill, but uncle Deane does not think Wakem would sell it.

COMMENT

The meeting between the brother and sister echoes the scene in Book One when Tom fetches Maggie from the attic and they share a cake in reconciliation (p. 403).

TEMPTATION AND RESCUE

Tom's treatment of Maggie is humiliating and reminds us of their childhood.

Tom can make her unhappy, he criticises her flighty behaviour (p. 401) without understanding the needs in her nature, but there is still much affection between them.

Tom's hard work has brought success: he might be able to buy the Mill. Although he does not seem happy, he does have an outlet for his feelings in his ambitions. In contrast Maggie has no such outlet, as it is a man's world.

GLOSSARY
glumpish sad

Pelley's bank the bank had failed and Tom warned his uncle, saving the firm money

BOOK SIX: CHAPTERS 6–8: ATTRACTION AND JEALOUSY

The river motif recalls the sense of Maggie's fate.

Maggie is introduced to society and the life of a lady, which she thoroughly enjoys after all the years of suffering. She likes being admired, but Eliot warns us that her destiny awaits (p. 411). She enjoys Stephen's company without acknowledging the attraction between them. On the evening that Lucy goes out, Stephen comes to bring some music and is alone with Maggie. It is clear that they are falling in love, although Stephen is angry at his confused feelings.

Philip still loves Maggie: he is bitter that she does not love him.

Next morning Philip calls and Maggie is emotional, recalling her childhood feelings and pity for him. She remembers his remark about taking a lover from Lucy and realises what is happening with Stephen. Stephen arrives and Philip sings a song which tells of his love for Maggie, but observing Stephen's behaviour with Maggie suspects that they are in love. Mr Deane speaks about business with Philip, and Lucy gets his permission to tell Philip about the plan to buy Dorlcote Mill.

Lucy tells Philip about the plan, and he sees it as a way to win Maggie. He tells his father about his love for

Wakem is more flexible than expected. Maggie and that he wants to marry her. After some initial anger, Wakem's fatherly affection surfaces and he gives Philip permission to marry and agrees to sell the Mill.

COMMENT The narrative tension (see Literary Terms) increases as feelings grow. Stephen's visit to see Maggie alone, Lucy's blindness to their love and Philip's suspicions build up a threat of discovery. Stephen knows it is madness (p. 418) but cannot resist.

Lucy's well-intentioned words with her father and Philip about the Mill increase the tension through dramatic irony (see Literary Terms): we know Maggie's true feelings, and that she will not want to marry Philip, although Lucy believes otherwise, and Philip hopes she will.

There is a difference in the sisterly affection Maggie feels for Philip, and the strong attraction she feels for Stephen, the smouldering passion as Maggie takes Stephen's arm (p. 417) shows the sexual nature of their feelings. Stephen's attractiveness contrasts with Philip's deformity, even kind-hearted Lucy is 'shocked' (p. 421) by the physical contrast between Maggie and Philip.

GLOSSARY gaucherie awkwardness
reticules ladies' handbags
minion favourite
monomania obsession
canterbury low open-topped piece of furniture for holding music and books

BOOK SIX: CHAPTERS 9–11: GROWING FEELINGS

At the charity bazaar Maggie's simple beauty attracts much male attention. Lucy is happy that her scheme about the Mill has worked. Wakem talks pleasantly to

Stephen and Maggie attempt to stay apart: they are trying to resist each other.

Maggie, and then Stephen approaches her. He speaks entreatingly to her but she will not reply. Stephen realises Philip is watching them, suddenly understands that there was some old attachment between him and Maggie and goes to speak to him. Philip shows that he knows about Stephen's feelings for Maggie, and they leave. Maggie is upset, but is comforted when Dr Kenn, the vicar, comes to speak to her and promises help if she needs it.

Maggie is trying to escape from her confused feelings.

Lucy has told Maggie about the plan to buy the Mill, but she is shocked when Maggie tells her that she is taking a new job very soon. She uses Tom as an excuse not to marry Philip.

At the Guests' party, the music and dancing help Maggie to forget her troubles. Stephen tries to quench his feelings, knowing that Philip is in love with Maggie, but feels repulsed by Philip's deformity. He eventually approaches Maggie, they walk outside together and, in a mad impulse, Stephen kisses Maggie's arm. She feels humiliated and runs from him.

Relieved that the spell between her and Stephen is broken, she meets Philip next morning and

explains that because of Tom, she will never marry
him.

Stephen is prepared Four days later Maggie is at her poor aunt Moss's when
to cross the social Stephen arrives. He tries to make Maggie accept him,
boundaries between saying he is suffering without her. She refuses, saying
himself and their love would be poisoned by the hurt it caused
Maggie: preparing others. He leaves and she cries at what she has had to
for the elopement. give up.

C OMMENT   Maggie attracts attention at the bazaar, just as later she
will attract gossip about her conduct. Dr Kenn's
promise to help her (p. 447) will also be important. Her
wish to die rather to continue suffering (p. 462) is
repeated at the end of the book.

It is part of Maggie's attraction to Stephen grows, but she struggles
Maggie's nature to hard against the temptation: she
want attention
and love.   • takes a new teaching post
                • tries not to talk to Stephen
                • runs from him when he kisses her
                • will not consider him as a lover

By kissing her, Stephen partly breaks the bounds of
acceptable behaviour, it would be considered too
forward and improper. Maggie's reaction is that he
thinks she would allow immoral behaviour, but she is
still quite conventional in her morality.

Maggie's excuse for not marrying Philip, Tom's
disapproval, is made to both Lucy and Philip. Whereas
Lucy believes her, Philip is sensitive and knows Maggie
well enough to have his doubts.

GLOSSARY   **canonicals** splendid clothing, usually used in connection with
             church vestments
             Caucasus mountainous region between the Black and Caspian
             Seas where the climate is harsh
             Parthenon the main temple on the Acropolis in Athens
             avatar god-like figure in earthly form

BOOK SIX: CHAPTERS 12–14: CARRIED AWAY

Maggie still wants Tom's affection and approval.

At aunt Pullet's tea-party Lucy tells Maggie that Wakem wants Tom to take over the Mill straightaway, hoping that this will persuade Maggie not to go away again to teach. The aunts also disapprove of Maggie's plan. When Tom arrives and is greeted by Maggie, the aunts talk of the linen they plan to give him. Lucy tells Tom about Philip's role in the recovery of the Mill, but Tom is still as prejudiced against him as ever and Lucy's words rekindle his suspicions about his sister's intentions.

The reference to the legend of St Ogg recalls the river motif

Maggie and Stephen both seem depressed but resigned to separation. They meet at Mr Deane's but rarely speak. Lucy arranges a boating trip to Luckreth for the four friends the next day, but Stephen rudely refuses to go. Next day, Philip, who has observed Maggie's and Stephen's mutual feelings, is too ill to go on the boat and sends Stephen instead. Lucy has arranged to go to Luckreth in her father's carriage, planning to leave Maggie and Philip alone, but it is Maggie and Stephen who go on the trip instead. Maggie is carried along in a dreamy, passive state, and does not realise they have gone past Luckreth and will be unable to return that night. Stephen pleads with her to elope with him, and at last they are picked up by a Dutch vessel and Maggie falls asleep, exhausted.

After a dream about the Virgin of St Ogg's and her friends, Maggie awakes and decides she must return. She thinks of what is morally right, not hurting Philip and Lucy, and leaves Stephen.

COMMENT   Maggie's relationship with Stephen, and her renunciation of him, is the culmination of all the influences we have seen on her character. We watch her make choices that we understand because we have seen her grow and mature.

The humorous presentation of the Dodson aunts reminds us of their disapproval of Maggie's unconventional behaviour, just as when she was a child.

Lucy's scheme inadvertently hardens Tom's feelings towards Philip, and makes him mistrust Maggie. The continuing sense of vendetta and prejudice keeps up the **narrative tension** (see Literary Terms).

Ironically Lucy had tried to put Maggie and Philip together. The river trip is presented as a coincidental final opportunity for the lovers to meet. Maggie is seen as passively borne along by a 'stronger presence' (p. 476), 'dimly conscious'. The idea of being carried along and taken against her will keeps her innocent, and her dream, in which she is the Virgin of St Ogg's, recalls the fact that she is still pure, even though society may condemn her. She acts to prevent harm to others rather than to fit the rules of society (p. 490), and we sympathise with her difficult decision which is based on her fidelity to her 'sacred ties' which are the affections of the past (p. 487).

GLOSSARY   **millennium** a thousand-year period of future happiness
cockatrices mythical serpents
nectar the wine of the ancient gods
native natural

BOOK SEVEN: CHAPTERS 1 AND 2: DISGRACE

Tom's triumph at getting the Mill is spoilt by Maggie's disgrace. Five days later Tom looks out from the Mill where he now lives and sees Maggie approaching, looking for refuge, although she expects his disapproval. He casts her out and condemns her, mentioning Lucy's suffering and Maggie's weakness. Surprisingly, Mrs Tulliver chooses to go with Maggie and they go to Bob Jakin's house, hoping for lodgings. Aware something is amiss he welcomes them and shows them his baby who he and his wife want to name Maggie. She asks him to send word to Dr Kenn, but learns his wife has just died.

TEMPTATION AND RESCUE

The rules of society St Ogg's would have been much happier if Stephen and
condemn Maggie, Maggie had married and returned after a few months,
although it was but everyone believes that Stephen came to his senses
Stephen who was just in time, changed his mind and sent Maggie back.
at fault. Stephen, who is in Holland, writes to his father,
explaining what really happened. Maggie is not worried
by public opinion, but concerned for Lucy, who is ill.
She visits Dr Kenn and tells him the whole story. He
understands and approves her motives, but warns her
that others will not. She asks him to help her find a job
and he agrees.

COMMENT   The **ironic** (see Literary Terms) reference to religion,
when the gossips hope that God will 'have mercy on'
Maggie (p. 504) while they themselves show none,
shows criticism of the harsh way in which Maggie is
Tom's harshness in received. Eliot disapproved of judging by a fixed set of
refusing her a rules, as 'men of maxims' (p. 510) do, preferring to look
home seems very at each case with sympathy.
cruel: Bob again
shows kindness. There is a difference between appearance and reality:
Maggie is still a virgin and has tried to behave in the
best way, as Dr Kenn realises. The letter from Stephen
confirms Maggie's innocence, but people are too ready
to condemn her.

GLOSSARY   **the warmest department** hell
              make no jaw keep quiet
              trousseau wedding outfit
              casuists people who deal with moral problems

BOOK SEVEN: CHAPTERS 3–5 AND CONCLUSION: RESCUE

Notice the contrast Surprisingly, Mrs Glegg refuses to believe ill of Maggie,
between Tom's doing her family duty by defending her when she learns
and Mrs Glegg's the contents of Stephen's letter and offering her a
response to home. Lucy is a little better, but Maggie is worried
Maggie's about Philip. She receives a letter from him in which he
situation. writes of his belief in her and his continuing love.

Maggie is overwhelmed by guilt at the pain she has caused.

Dr Kenn, unable to persuade anyone in St Ogg's to employ Maggie, takes her on as governess to his children, but the gossips disapprove, fearing he will marry her. Maggie hears that Lucy is to go away, and is sad that she will not see her, but, quite unexpectedly, Lucy secretly comes to see her and the cousins take a loving farewell.

Stephen knows that his own pain might persuade Maggie to accept him.

On a rainy night in September, Maggie is sitting alone in her room at Bob Jakin's, having been asked to leave by Dr Kenn, who had been forced to do so by the gossips. She is upset because she fears she must leave St Ogg's and she has had a letter from Stephen, pleading with her to let him come back to her. After a terrible struggle, Maggie destroys the letter and as she does so, she realises the river is in flood. She helps Bob to safety, then sets out to rescue Tom. Miraculously, she reaches the Mill and Tom climbs into the boat.

As they set out to make sure Lucy is safe, their boat is hit by the wreckage of some machinery – it sinks and they drown in each other's arms.

TEMPTATION AND RESCUE

Five years later, their joint grave is still visited by Philip, alone, and by Stephen who later marries Lucy.

COMMENT   This final section brings the novel movingly to a close with a sense of fulfilment and reconciliation:

We recognise that Philip had a much better understanding of Maggie than Stephen.

- Philip's letter shows his knowledge of Maggie's character, the 'vibration of chords' which he did not feel in Stephen (p. 514) and he generously forgives her
- Lucy and Maggie are reconciled in what will be their final embrace (p. 523)
- Maggie overcomes her final temptation to respond to Stephen's letter (p. 528)
- Tom and Maggie are eternally united as they drown and are buried together

The evil of gossip and the lack of common humanity is shown in the harsh treatment of Maggie, who is innocent of wrongdoing but is hounded out of her job

Even Dr Kenn considers that the best outcome would be for the pair to marry.

with Dr Kenn by the women who judge her. Marriage to Stephen would have caused others pain and that, for Maggie, was the ultimate evil. It would, however, have been more socially acceptable, reflecting the injustice of a fixed set of rules.

The tumult of the river brings 'a great calm' to Maggie.

The flood is the culmination of the river **motif**. It is **cathartic** (see Literary Terms), ending Maggie's suffering after her final renunciation of Stephen and reunites the brother and sister. Tom experiences a revelation in the boat (p. 533) that Maggie has miraculously brought to the Mill. He realises that he has been mistaken in his harsh judgements and the pet, childhood, name 'Magsie' reflects the renewed affection. As they die, they clasp each other and it is as if the blissful times when they were together in childhood are extended into eternity (p. 534).

GLOSSARY   **legatee** person who receives something from a will

Peter the disciple who denied Christ and afterwards regretted his weakness

A Identify the speaker.

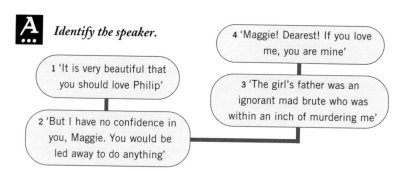

1 'It is very beautiful that you should love Philip'

2 'But I have no confidence in you, Maggie. You would be led away to do anything'

3 'The girl's father was an ignorant mad brute who was within an inch of murdering me'

4 'Maggie! Dearest! If you love me, you are mine'

Identify the person 'to whom' this comment refers.

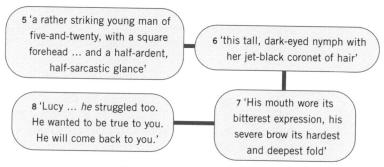

5 'a rather striking young man of five-and-twenty, with a square forehead ... and a half-ardent, half-sarcastic glance'

6 'this tall, dark-eyed nymph with her jet-black coronet of hair'

7 'His mouth wore its bitterest expression, his severe brow its hardest and deepest fold'

8 'Lucy ... *he* struggled too. He wanted to be true to you. He will come back to you.'

Check your answers on page 84.

B Consider these issues.

a The river motif throughout the novel and how it prepares us for the ending.

b The way in which we understand Maggie because we have seen her growing up – note the similarities and links to the childhood section. Do you find her likeable?

c The theme of judgement and false religion: what do you think of the way in which St Ogg's treats Maggie? Is she guilty?

d The reasons for Maggie's decisions to marry neither Philip nor Stephen: do you think she is right?

e The people who show understanding and kindness to Maggie: some are expected e.g. Bob, others are surprising e.g. Mrs Glegg. List them and their reasons.

f The ending: did you find it satisfying? Realistic? Disappointing? Consider the reasons for your answer.

PART THREE

COMMENTARY

THEMES

Eliot was determined to write realistically about ordinary people, shunning the **melodramatic** (see Literary Terms) style common in novels of the time. Her subject, a young girl whose childhood experiences reflect her own, lets her explore the idea that ordinary people suffer, and are judged severely, because of circumstances and their own personalities. Although her characters create some of the problems for themselves, they are also caught up in events, as shown by the river **motif** (see Literary Terms) which reflects the powerlessness of man against nature.

THE INFLUENCE OF CHILDHOOD

In the early part of *The Mill on the Floss*, Eliot draws heavily on her own childhood and her relationship with Isaac, her adored elder brother (see George Eliot's Background). Originally she wanted to call the novel 'Sister Maggie' which shows the importance of the relationship with Tom. In particular, the rift between Eliot and Isaac is used in the relationship between Maggie and Tom. Eliot shows her belief that one's roots are vital in one's development as a character, which must have made her own situation even more difficult to bear. She wrote a series of sonnets called *Brother and Sister* in which she states that from those days spent with her brother she learnt 'the meaning that gives words a soul', and that those days 'Were but my growing self'.

As boy and man Tom is harsh to Maggie. As a child, Maggie seeks for love from Tom, but he is more likely to reject and punish her than embrace her, for example the quarrel over the jam tart (Book One, Chapter 6).

Experiencing Maggie's growing up helps us understand her and sympathise with her.

When Tom discovers her secret meetings with Philip (Book Five, Chapter 5), and when she seeks refuge at the Mill having left Stephen (Book Seven, Chapter 1), Tom is equally stern and unforgiving. The lack of love from Tom helps us to understand Maggie's need to find it elsewhere, and explains her attraction to Stephen and Philip, who offer it to her.

Maggie's family compound her problems. Mrs Tulliver worries about her wildness (Book One, Chapter 2), the Dodson aunts disapprove of her (Book One, Chapter 7), Tom seeks to control her, even her beloved father sees her as 'too 'cute for a woman'. Their attitudes make her seem isolated and frustrated as a child and this continues into adulthood.

Childhood ties influence Maggie:
- She fears Tom's disapproval throughout, which affects her choices
- She is partly attracted to Philip by memories of her childish affection for him
- She struggles against Philip's suggestion that they meet secretly because she feels bound by family loyalty (Book Five, Chapter 3)
- She resists Stephen because of the pain it would cause those to whom she is bound by ties of the past, i.e. Tom, Lucy, Philip (Book Six, Chapter 14)

Childhood influences are also mentioned by Eliot herself, who states that we love the world because we had 'our childhood in it' (p. 38) and childhood is seen as having 'golden gates' (p. 193), reflecting the happiness of this time in most people's lives.

ORDINARY PEOPLE AND RESTRICTIVE LIVES

As already mentioned, despite being set in 1829, the novel really reflects the attitudes of the early part of the Victorian era, attitudes which the author herself had to suffer. *The Mill on the Floss* shows very clearly how Victorian restrictions affected intelligent women, like Maggie, who were capable of so much more.

Eliot focuses on ordinary country people, which reflects the influence of her favourite poet, Wordsworth, who also wrote about country folk. She recreates the simple monotony of life in a small town just before industrialisation, to show the limited ideas and restricted opinions against which impetuous, intelligent Maggie struggles.

Eliot apologises for the oppressive feeling caused by her picture of this 'sordid life' (p. 276) but says it is necessary to understand the way in which the most humble souls have their tragedies. Here it is Maggie who, 'thirsty for all knowledge' (p. 238), finds the world outside her books lacking in love and life.

The lack of understanding and freedom for Maggie reflects the inequality women faced at that time.

- They must not be intelligent, like Maggie (Book One, Chapter 2). Mrs Tulliver was chosen because she was not clever (Book One, Chapter 3) and it is Tom who must be educated even though he is less clever.
- Appearance and quietness are highly valued qualities, Lucy's behaviour is commended by the aunts (Book One, Chapter 9).
- They are dependent on men: Tom punishes Maggie, he can work in business and accumulate money and power, Maggie must sit passively or at the most work as a governess to earn her keep. Indeed, the family disapprove of all Maggie's efforts to earn money.
- Wakem says that 'We don't ask what a woman does, we ask whom she belongs to' (p. 436), reflecting the attitude that women were property.
- Stephen is attracted to Lucy because she is a 'little darling' rather than an equal (p. 379).

- Stephen's wealth and the fact that he is a man allows him to flee abroad, while Maggie must return to St Ogg's and face her disgrace.

In the narrow, prejudiced world of St Ogg's, with its constant disapproval of differences, an explosive nature like Maggie's is bound to suffer. Philip also suffers from prejudice against his physical differences. Being also lonely and misunderstood, he understands Maggie's suffering best, as his generously forgiving letter (p. 514) shows.

RELIGION AND MORAL JUDGEMENTS

Eliot shows that forgiveness and mercy should be at the centre of religion.

Eliot presents St Ogg's attitude to religion with considerable **irony** (see Literary Terms): the inhabitants have a narrow view of Christianity – church is for Sunday and what is preached from the pulpit is not allowed to interfere with their everyday lives:

- There is 'little trace of religion' in St Ogg's (p. 276) and certainly their attitudes are far from Christian
- The revenge **motif** (see Literary Terms) – Tulliver dictates a curse for Tom to write in the family Bible with no sense that it is wrong (p. 271)
- St Ogg's judgement of Maggie when she returns from Stephen: the cruel and hypocritical gossips pretend to hope that 'God would have mercy on her' (p. 504)
- Tom regards Maggie as immoral, although he is prepared to continue his father's vendetta which is morally wrong

Maggie has religious feelings as shown by her conversion after reading *The Imitation of Christ*, and Dr Kenn recognises her struggle to give up Stephen as real spiritual conflict (p. 509). It is, however, **ironic** (see Literary Terms) that he also believes that marriage to Stephen is Maggie's best option, although for Maggie it

is impossible since she could not find happiness
through causing pain to others.

Eliot suggests that judging a person by a fixed set of
rules is wrong – each case deserves individual and
sympathetic judgement (p. 510). Our insight into
Maggie's character lets us judge her innocence: she may
break society's rules but she keeps to her own strong
moral code and her intentions are good even though
the outcome looks bad.

THE RIVER AND REVENGE MOTIFS

Eliot set the book in Lincolnshire, an area known for
flooding, to ensure that the story was as realistic as
possible.

The river **motif** (see Literary Terms) recurs throughout
the book, from the first chapter, where the little girl is
seen beside the water, to the final tragedy, where she
drowns:

- Mrs Tulliver is worried that Maggie will drown
  (p. 34)
- Tom discusses a flood with Bob Jakin (p. 47)
- Eliot mentions floods on the River Rhône (p. 275)
- The legend of St Ogg concerns a boatman (p. 116)
- Stephen's and Maggie's boat trip (p. 476)

References to the river motif are strategically placed
throughout the novel, and they have several effects on
the narrative:

- They prepare us for the final flood and tragic
  drowning
- They suggest the power of nature and a sense of
  Man's helplessness against fate
- They create an impression of time moving on
- The dream of the legend of St Ogg's (p. 482)
  links Maggie to the Madonna, emphasising her
  purity

• It gives the narrative a dignity and sense of
significance through its link to history

The revenge **motif** which centres around the enmity
between Tulliver and Wakem builds **narrative tension**
(see Literary Terms) and gives a focus to the rift
between Tom and Maggie.

Tom is ordered by his father to write in the Bible that
he will seek revenge on Wakem (p. 271). Tom does so
willingly, much to Maggie's horror. She sees it for what
it is, morally wrong, but Tom accepts it as his duty to
his father. This perpetuates the vendetta beyond
Tulliver's death after his foolish attack on Wakem
(p. 363). The promise of revenge is what really divides
Tom and Maggie on the issue of whether she should
meet Philip, and makes the threat of the discovery of
their meetings the more dangerous (p. 344).

EDUCATION

A minor theme is Eliot's criticism of the way in which
schooling was organised at that time, and the
unsuitability of the kind of education received by Tom
at the hands of Mr Stelling. Tom suffers because Mr
Stelling is unintelligent, greedy and self-seeking,
preferring to try to teach Tom Latin and geometry even
though he is clearly unsuited to it (p. 140). Eliot
comments that education was then 'a matter of luck –
usually ill luck' (p. 169), as seen by the random way
Riley recommends Stelling (p. 23) to Mr Tulliver.

It is **ironic** (see Literary Terms) that Tom's expensive
education prejudices Mr Deane against him when he
goes seeking a job. Tom's promise that he will soon
forget it all reflects Eliot's low opinion of education that
does not suit the individual pupil – notice how it suits
Philip and how interested Maggie is in Tom's lessons
(Book Two, Chapter 1).

STRUCTURE

The Mill on the Floss is divided into seven books:
- The first two deal with Maggie's childhood
- The third with her father's bankruptcy
- The fourth and fifth with her experience of poverty and deprivation up to her father's death
- The sixth with her temptation
- The seventh with her disgrace and death

The reader experiences the events that shape Maggie's character in the order in which they happen.

The structure is **chronological** (see Literary Terms) with the exception of Book Three, Chapter 1 which explains the details of Tulliver's bankruptcy. As a result, having seen life through her eyes as a child, we understand the choices she makes as an adult. To speed up the process, there are several leaps in time, such as at the end of Book Two, when we are told that Maggie is now thirteen, and at the beginning of Book Six, when two years have passed.

To help to keep the plot believable and dynamic, Eliot uses repetition and echoes. The river motif (see Themes) prepares the reader for the ending and enriches the narrative with a sense of history, and the revenge motif (see Themes) creates a sense of **narrative tension** (see Literary Terms) and threat.

The author creates a sense of balance and contrast between her characters:
- Bob's warmth and Mr Glegg's meanness
- Tom's inflexibility and Philip's understanding
- Maggie's innocence and the cruel gossips
- Aunt Moss's poverty and the Dodsons' wealth

Most of the action is seen through Maggie's eyes.

The central focus is on Maggie and this maintains the reader's sympathy for her suffering. Even when she is not central to the action, as when Tom goes to school in Book Two, Maggie's visits keep her in view and allow her character to develop. The dramatic ending is a shock, despite the river motif, as the character with whom we have most sympathy dies.

MAGGIE

Intelligent
Impetuous
Passionate
Hungry for
affection
Courageous
Naive

This hunger for
culture tempts her
to meet Philip
again in Book
Five, Chapter 3.

Maggie is a sensitive, passionate girl who is condemned throughout her life for what she is. The narrow confines of the male-dominated society in which she lives is prejudiced against those who will not conform. We are introduced to her as a 'small mistake of nature' (p. 9) and her loneliness is shown throughout the novel, as in the attempt to escape from her family's disapproval by running away to the gypsies (p. 103) and later when she is alone in the boat during the flood: 'Oh God where am I? Which is the way home?' (p. 530).

An intelligent, loving child, she is very dependent on her brother because he is the first thing she remembers (p. 313). She longs for him to come home from school (p. 29), but is hurt by his punishment for the death of his rabbits (p. 32). The pattern of her relationship with her brother continues into adulthood, when she is just as hungry for love and Tom is just as severe, as when he discovers she has been meeting Philip (p. 349).

Maggie is loyal to her father, who loves and defends his 'little wench'. She is more concerned than either her mother or Tom when he is ill (p. 207). She shares his impetuous nature, as when she cut off her hair (p. 61) and when she pushed Lucy in the mud (p. 99), but she regrets her actions and always wishes she had done something different (p. 50) and she is against the idea of revenge (p. 271).

She suffers after her father's bankruptcy because of the loss of her books and music, but her renunciation of these things and more general pleasure after reading *The Imitation of Christ* helps her at a difficult time. Later it will give her moral strength to resist Stephen's temptation.

Maggie's loving nature draws her to the crippled Philip (p. 185). Although her feelings for him are sisterly, she

Maggie's need for love makes her vulnerable.

cannot bring herself to hurt him with the truth when she says she cannot marry him, blaming Tom's disapproval instead (p. 455). She comes under Stephen's power, although she does her best to resist, and finally succeeds by burning his last letter (p. 528). She knows that she cannot enjoy happiness that will bring pain to others, i.e. Lucy and Philip. Whatever the town might think, Maggie is innocent, as her link to the Virgin of St Ogg's shows.

Tom, who does not appreciate the complexity of her nature, accuses her of being weak and lacking in willpower (p. 401). The reader, however, sees events through her eyes and hears her inner voice, so understanding her flexibility and the courageous love she has, which enables her to give up her happiness for others and to risk her life rescuing her stern brother. Her death is a tragic waste, but she finds joy in the eternal embrace of the brother who finally recognises her true worth.

TOM

Insensitive
Severe
Inflexible
Hard-working
Arrogant

Tom is seen as a typical boy (p. 29): physical, self-satisfied and unsentimental. His harsh treatment of adoring Maggie in Book One makes him seem cruel and unfeeling, but his suffering during Mr Stelling's education makes him more human (p. 141). He treats Maggie as inferior because she is a girl (p. 151) and he regards himself as superior by his very maleness.

His loyalty to his family matches Maggie's, but it takes a different form. Brother and sister are united at times of family tragedy, such as Tulliver's death (p. 367), but unlike Maggie, Tom blames his father for his stubborn misjudgements (p. 206) and is prepared to shoulder the burden of revenge which Maggie rejects. The revenge is morally wrong, but Tom always believes he does the right thing (p. 50) and then judges Maggie's behaviour by his own inflexible rules.

His cruelty and lack of patience is shown in his
treatment of those weaker than himself, he refuses to
give Maggie help and a home when she needs it most
(p. 496) and he considers it fair when he humiliates
Philip sadistically (p. 353), but he is forced to take adult
responsibility early and he seems lonely, with only his
work for company (p. 408).

On the positive side, he shows nobility when he follows
his father's wishes not to recall the Moss's £300, and
pride in his hard-working determination to repay the
family debts. He achieves his father's wish: he gets the
Mill back. He also seems finally to recognise Maggie's
worth when she comes to rescue him (p. 533) and they
are reconciled.

Mr tulliver

Stubborn
Impetuous
Warm-hearted
Quick-tempered
Loving to
Maggie

Mr Tulliver is presented with **irony** (see Literary
Terms) and affection. He is not very intelligent, yet
takes pride that he has a wife less clever than himself
(p. 16) and that Maggie's cleverness comes from his
side. Maggie may have her father's impetuosity, as
when he insists on paying back Mrs Glegg's money
(p. 129), and Tom has his stubborn, vengeful prejudices
against Wakem (p. 271), but her intelligence is certainly
not inherited!

He wants Tom to be educated but has little idea what
that involves (p. 137). He takes pride in his Mill but
puts it in jeopardy by going to law. He is warm and
affectionate to his family and protective of Maggie, as
when she cuts her hair (p. 66), but he knows he has

It is ironic that
Tulliver hopes that
his son (Tom) will
be as kind to his
sister (Maggie).

ruined her marriage chances (p. 299). He is proud of
Tom's success (p. 361), but loses his temper and attacks
Wakem (p. 363). He is also generous to his sister, not
demanding the £300 he lent her (p. 82). He is naively
convinced all will be well even after the lost lawsuit

(p. 198), but then is forced to become Wakem's
employee (p. 270).

Tulliver has many faults and is largely responsible for
his ruin, but he is a warm, likeable character in a
'puzzling world' (p. 198) who is brought pitiably low in
his apathy (p. 226) and death. Maggie's affection for
her father contributes to our sympathy for him.

Mrs tulliver

Foolish

Fond of
possessions

Despairing of
Maggie as a child

Finally loyal to
Maggie

Mrs Tulliver is a rather pathetic figure, chosen by her
husband because she was not clever (p. 16) and yet she
has a sense of marrying below her because she is a
Dodson (p. 41). The youngest of the sisters, she feels
bullied when they come, especially by the eldest, Jane
Glegg (p. 52), probably reflecting the situation when
she was a child. She is ashamed of Maggie, who is so
brown and wild (p. 59), although she loves Tom, who
is, she thinks, more of a Dodson (p. 8).

It is Mrs Tulliver's foolish interventions that hasten
disaster: her words persuade Tulliver to repay Mrs
Glegg (p. 129), and until her visit to Wakem he had
not thought of buying the Mill (p. 254). She also tells
Tulliver that the Mill is Wakem's (p. 265).

When they must sell up, she seems more concerned for
her linen than her ill husband (p. 205), and this causes
a rift with Maggie. But at the end, with a true 'mother's
instinct', she stands by her daughter, leaving the Mill
when Tom casts Maggie out (p. 498).

The dodson relations

The aunts are
gently mocked by
Eliot.

Mrs Tulliver's sisters have all married better than
her – and they never let her forget it. They feel superior
because of the Dodson traditions and they represent
solid middle-class respectability. They are mean in

their help to the Tullivers as Maggie tells them
(p. 218).

Mr and Mrs Glegg	Jane Glegg, the eldest and most argumentative of Maggie's aunts, speaks her mind and gives advice even when it is not wanted (p. 52). Her criticism of the plan for Tom's education seems like interfering (p. 68) but in the end she is proved right. Her hidden store of unworn lace (p. 50) represents the 'having' nature of the Dodsons. She joins the other Dodsons in a mean-spirited response to the Tullivers' downfall (p. 215).

Her relationship with her husband is humorously drawn
(p. 123) as she manages to make an argument for
herself and he takes refuge in the garden. Mr Glegg is
mean but he has some pleasant qualities and he is quite
fond of his wife's odd ways.

Tulliver's downfall is not caused by aunt Glegg
demanding her money, she had decided to let him keep
it (p. 127), and the same sense of family makes her one
of Maggie's few defenders after she returns from
Stephen (p. 511).

Mr and Mrs Deane	The Deanes are the wealthiest of the Dodson relations and Lucy's parents. Susan Deane dies when Lucy is seventeen: Mr Deane, a self-made man, works for Guest and Co. and helps Tom to his first job. He is linked to the increasing industrialisation that is occurring in St Ogg's as he is making money rapidly, but they are not generous people, although Mr Deane takes Mrs Tulliver in to act as their housekeeper after Mrs Deane's death. Mr Deane also reveals the contents of Stephen's letter which excuses Maggie's behaviour (p. 511).
Mr and Mrs Pullet	Sophie Pullet is a hypochondriac and an amusing caricature, always in tears, and so house-proud that Tom and Maggie cannot wipe their feet on her mat

(p. 86). Mr Pullet is seen as a bit of a fool, always offering peppermints. When they are young Tom and Maggie find his musical snuff box fascinating.

LUCY DEANE   Lucy, a contrast to Maggie, is wealthy, fair and neat. Maggie likes her but, as a child, feels jealous of her and pushes her in the mud (p. 99). Maggie mentions her dislike of blond heroines to Philip (p. 339) and it certainly seems as if Lucy has it all.

Lucy's mother dies when she is seventeen and Mrs Tulliver becomes the Deanes' housekeeper. Although Lucy is a lady of leisure she is not spoilt, as she shows affection and is generous in her impulses to help Maggie and her mother (p. 378). She tries to help by getting Philip's father to sell the Mill (p. 432), but her judgements are not all sound: she angers Tom by mentioning Philip's role (p. 468) and is blind to Maggie's and Stephen's love because she believes Maggie loves Philip.

Well-behaved
Good-natured
Trusting
Affectionate

She suffers at Stephen's betrayal, but forgives Maggie in a warm, genuine manner (p. 522).

PHILIP WAKEM

Philip, deformed after a childhood accident, loves Maggie but is sensitive to the fact that she is not attracted to him – there are frequent references to his almost feminine manner. He is similar to her in mind and understanding but it is his tragedy to be excluded from normal life because of his physical deformity.

He is contrasted to the hearty, physical Tom and to handsome Stephen, but it is clear that he has a beautiful nature: at school he understands Tom's fears about his foot (p. 183) and later he shows Maggie generous forgiveness in his letter (p. 514).

Crippled
Sensitive
Intelligent
An outsider

He reflects the world of culture of which Maggie is starved, bringing her books (p. 339), and he turns her from the sterile road of renunciation (p. 309). He is humiliated by Tom's cruel attack (p. 353) and jealous that her love for Stephen is mutual, but in loving Maggie he has found his one fulfilment, and he walks the Red Deeps with his memories of her (p. 535).

STEPHEN GUEST

In Book Six, Stephen is linked to Lucy though not yet engaged to her. His father owns Guest and Co. and he has chosen Lucy because she is slightly beneath him (p. 379), both socially and intellectually. He is lazy by comparison with Tom (p. 375), although clearly has little need to work hard, and he is rather shallow until he meets Maggie.

Elegant and
handsome
Lazy and
wealthy
Passionate
Conceited

He is immediately attracted to Maggie because she is so challenging (p. 385) and finds it impossible to resist her, kissing her arm (p. 453) in a clear breach of etiquette. He represents a world of ease and love for deprived Maggie: he is her great temptation. From his pleas at her aunt Gritty's (p461), his persuasion when their boat drifts too far (p. 490) and his final impassioned letter (p. 526) it is clear that he has deep feelings for her, but his conduct is questionable and was highly criticised when the book was published. His letter to his father proves Maggie's innocence, however, and he takes all the blame (p. 508). He marries Lucy some time after Maggie's death.

LAWYER WAKEM

Philip's father and Tulliver's enemy: he defeats Tulliver in law then buys the Mill and employs him. He is not the ogre Tulliver believes, he shows greater flexibility to his son's wishes than we suspect Tulliver ever would.

BOB JAKIN

Warm

Sharp

Devoted to

Maggie

As a boy, Bob scared birds from Tulliver's crops, and argues with Tom over a halfpenny (p. 48), but picks up the knife he throws after Tom, valuing it.

He is from a lower class than the other characters but, unlike the Dodsons, he is generous after Tulliver's ruin, offering all he has (p. 243), buying books for Maggie (p. 287), helping Tom in business (p. 317) and giving Maggie a home when Tom will not (p. 499). He seems to be there whenever Maggie or Tom are in need.

He is a humorous character with his lively dialect, sharp in persuading Mrs Glegg to buy from his pack (p. 329) and comic with his dog and his tiny wife, but he shows Eliot's belief that a humble exterior can contain a noble, chivalrous soul (p. 290).

THE TULLIVER RELATIONS

Mr and Mrs
Moss

Tulliver's sister, Margaret (Gritty) has married beneath her: Mr Moss is a poor farmer and in debt to her brother for £300. They have eight children. Aunt Moss is warm, kind to Maggie and speaks well of her whereas the other aunts only criticise (p. 78). She is also the most genuinely concerned relative when Tulliver is ill (p. 219) and she shows a generosity the richer relations lack. Gritty is not failed by her brother as Tom fails Maggie – Tulliver cancels her debt at the time of his own hardship. Maggie loves her and goes to her after Stephen has kissed her.

DR KENN

The vicar of St Ogg's and a recent widower, he employs Maggie when the town condemns her, but pressured and shocked by the gossips' cruelty he has to send her away.

It is easy to identify a Victorian novel, the words and length of the sentences are very different from those in a modern book. *The Mill on the Floss* is full of descriptions to create atmosphere, with regional characters and places, and it also makes use of dialogue to add humour and contrast between people. Eliot also uses two other devices: an **authorial voice** (see Literary Terms) and the 'inner voices' of the characters.

Eliot was writing for a purpose: to explore the way moral judgements are made. To do this, she had to:

- Draw and contrast the characters to create balance and sharpen themes
- Describe the setting and atmosphere to give a backdrop to the action
- Let us hear the 'inner voice' of the characters' thoughts and decisions
- Tell us her opinions in an authorial voice to direct our ideas and opinions of her characters
- Use **symbolism** and **motifs** (see Literary Terms) to enrich the text

Dialogue
Look at Tom's conversation with Bob Jakin in Book 3, Chapter 6.

The realism of the dialogue and the variety of the **dialect** (see Literary Terms) add life to the characters. The unconscious humour in Mrs Tulliver's speech is amusing, the children's speech is convincing and Bob's warmth comes through in his talkative dialect, in contrast to the better-spoken but meaner Gleggs.

Creation of atmosphere

The historical setting of St Ogg's is described in such a way (p. 115) as to give it a conventional, oppressive atmosphere, a background which Maggie's nature cannot accept. The contrast between the hardships of Maggie's life, and Lucy's indulgent lifestyle is created by the description of the ball (pp. 449–50). The description of events is also atmospheric: the shadowy Red Deeps (pp. 304–5) are a perfect place for secret meetings and the flood scene is vividly drawn (pp. 530–1).

Inner voice   The use of a character's 'inner voice' lets us understand their thoughts and reasons. Philip's character is contrasted to Tom's when they first meet at the Stellings', but the boys' different reactions are shown through their thoughts rather than words (p. 167). We understand Maggie's reasons for her choices as we are shown her thought processes throughout, culminating in her resistance of Stephen's letter (p. 528).

Authorial   George Eliot also speaks directly to the reader at times,
voice   using an **authorial voice** or **tone** (see Literary Terms). As the **omniscient narrator** (see Literary Terms), she generally tells the story in an impersonal way, but occasionally she uses 'I' or 'me', so commenting on the morality of the actions and characters and directing our judgements, for example when she tells us not to judge Philip harshly (p. 338).

Symbolism and **motifs**, such as the river and revenge motifs (see Themes and Literary Terms) thread through the story, giving it tension and shape. In a lesser way, the dark shadows of the Red Deeps, and the place's name, give Maggie's meetings with Philip a sense of secrecy and danger (p. 305).

Irony and **satire** (see Literary Terms) are used in the treatment of characters to influence our opinions, e.g. the picture of the greedy Mr Stelling (pp. 168–9) and **dramatic irony** (see Literary Terms) is used when Lucy is unaware of the feeling between Maggie and Stephen.

PART FOUR

STUDY SKILLS

HOW TO USE QUOTATIONS

One of the secrets of success in writing essays is the way you use quotations. There are five basic principles:

- Put inverted commas at the beginning and end of the quotation
- Write the quotation exactly as it appears in the original
- Do not use a quotation that repeats what you have just written
- Use the quotation so that it fits into your sentence
- Keep the quotation as short as possible

Quotations should be used to develop the line of thought in your essays.

Your comment should not duplicate what is in your quotation. For example:

> Maggie tells Philip that the first thing she remembers as a child is holding her brother's hand in the quotation: 'the first thing I remember in my life is standing with Tom by the side of the Floss while he held my hand'.

Far more effective is to write:

> Tom has been important to Maggie from her early childhood, as shown when she says to Philip: 'the first thing I remember in my life is standing with Tom by the side of the Floss while he held my hand'.

However, the most sophisticated way of using the writer's words is to embed them into your sentence:

> Maggie's lifelong affection for Tom is conveyed by the way in which 'standing with Tom by the side of the Floss' is 'the first thing' she remembers.

When you use quotations in this way, you are demonstrating the ability to use text as evidence to support your ideas - not simply including words from the original to prove you have read it.

Coursework essay

Everyone writes differently. Work through the suggestions given here and adapt the advice to suit your own style and interests. This will improve your essay-writing skills and allow your personal voice to emerge.

The following points indicate in ascending order the skills of essay writing:
- Picking out one or two facts about the story and adding the odd detail
- Writing about the text by retelling the story
- Retelling the story and adding a quotation here and there
- Organising an answer which explains what is happening in the text and giving quotations to support what you write

....

- Writing in such a way as to show that you have thought about the intentions of the writer of the text and that you understand the techniques used
- Writing at some length, giving your viewpoint on the text and commenting by picking out details to support your views
- Looking at the text as a work of art, demonstrating clear critical judgement and explaining to the reader of your essay how the enjoyment of the text is assisted by literary devices, linguistic effects and psychological insights; showing how the text relates to the time when it was written

The dotted line above represents the division between lower and higher level grades. Higher-level performance begins when you start to consider your response as a reader of the text. The highest level is reached when you offer an enthusiastic personal response and show how this piece of literature is a product of its time.

Coursework
essay

Set aside an hour or so at the start of your work to plan what you have to do.

- List all the points you feel are needed to cover the task. Collect page references of information and quotations that will support what you have to say. A helpful tool is the highlighter pen: this saves painstaking copying and enables you to target precisely what you want to use.
- Focus on what you consider to be the main points of the essay. Try to sum up your argument in a single sentence, which could be the closing sentence of your essay. Depending on the essay title, it could be a statement about a character: The Tullivers' bankruptcy hardens Tom and he is forced to take on a more adult role. This increases his conflict with Maggie; an opinion about setting: St Ogg's is a small pre-industrial town on the brink of change. The community's fixed ideas on behaviour clash with Maggie's unconventional ways; or a judgement on a theme: Moral judgements are a major theme as Eliot believed that it was wrong to have a fixed set of rules: individuals, like Maggie, should be judged on their own merits.
- Make a short essay plan. Use the first paragraph to introduce the argument you wish to make. In the following paragraphs develop this argument with details, examples and other possible points of view. Sum up your argument in the last paragraph. Check you have answered the question.
- Write the essay, remembering all the time the central point you are making.
- On completion, go back over what you have written to eliminate careless errors and improve expression. Read it aloud to yourself, or, if you are feeling more confident, to a relative or friend.

If you can, try to type your essay, using a word processor. This will allow you to correct and improve your writing without spoiling its appearance.

Examination essay

The essay written in an examination often carries more marks than the coursework essay even though it is written under considerable time pressure.

In the revision period build up notes on various aspects of the text you are using. Fortunately, in acquiring this set of York Notes on *The Mill on the Floss*, you have made a prudent beginning! York Notes are set out to give you vital information and help you to construct your personal overview of the text.

Make notes with appropriate quotations about the key issues of the set text. Go into the examination knowing your text and having a clear set of opinions about it.

In most English Literature examinations you can take in copies of your set books. This in an enormous advantage although it may lull you into a false sense of security. Beware! There is simply not enough time in an examination to read the book from scratch.

In the examination

- Read the question paper carefully and remind yourself what you have to do.
- Look at the questions on your set texts to select the one that most interests you and mentally work out the points you wish to stress.
- Remind yourself of the time available and how you are going to use it.
- Briefly map out a short plan in note form that will keep your writing on track and illustrate the key argument you want to make.
- Then set about writing it.
- When you have finished, check through to eliminate errors.

To summarise,   • Know the text
these are the   • Have a clear understanding of and opinions on the storyline,
keys to success: characters, setting, themes and writer's concerns
               • Select the right material
               • Plan and write a clear response, continually bearing the question
                 in mind

Sample essay plan

A typical essay question on *The Mill on the Floss* is followed by a sample essay plan in note form. You will need to look back through the text to find quotations to support your points. Think about your own ideas – the sample answer is only a suggestion and you may wish to ignore it and produce your own. But it is always a good idea to plan out your thoughts first – it will save you time and help you to organise your ideas. Remember – try to answer the question!

How does the background of the novel affect Maggie's life and character?

Such a question anticipates quite a wide-ranging response. You will need to consider the time and the place in which she lived, her family influences and her nature, backing up your points with references to the text.

An outline of the answer could be like this:

Part One   Introduce your subject by:
             • Outlining Maggie's background – St Ogg's is a small
               pre-industrial town and Maggie's family is critical of
               her unconventional character
             • Effect on character – she is hurt by Tom's rejections
               which make her need affection
             • Effect on life – this need for love draws her to Philip
               and Stephen

Part Two   Develop the subject – explore why there is disapproval of Maggie, using short quotations to support your points.

Show how the various members of the family disapprove of her:
- Tom
- her mother
- her aunts

Show St Ogg's attitude:
- It is an old town with fixed ideas of right and wrong, it may be on the edge of change, but this is not yet reflected in the people's attitudes
- People make quick, wrong judgements and enjoy gossip
- The people are prejudiced. They lack understanding, pity and mercy

Look at her clash with restrictive Victorian and Dodson ideas about how young ladies should be – give examples (tip: Lucy is an ideal Victorian miss)

Part Three   The effect of disapproval on Maggie's character:
- Maggie receives no affection from her brother, the effect – she is hungry for love
- St Ogg's condemns Maggie after fleeing from Stephen, the effect – she is isolated, an outsider

The effect on her life:
- Maggie's need for warmth and culture draws her to Philip and makes her willing to risk meeting him
- Her isolation and need for affection increases the temptation to go to Stephen, so needs more strength to resist and makes her wish to die

Part Four   In the conclusion sum up the points you have already made. This is your opportunity to express your opinions, and provided you have explored all the influences and back your conclusions up from the text, your opinion is as valid as anyone else's.

FURTHER QUESTIONS

Make a plan as shown above and attempt these questions.

1 Maggie loves Tom but does Eliot portray Tom as a loveable character? Consider his behaviour towards Maggie, his father, his other relations and Philip, and look at his reaction to the bankruptcy. How were his attitudes typical of his time?

2 Philip and Maggie share similar fates – they are both outsiders due to prejudice. Look at the links between the two characters and the way Victorian society treats them.

3 How does Eliot bring us to understand the decisions Maggie makes to resist Stephen's love? Look at the childhood section, her renunciation stage and social attitudes of the time.

4 Look at the use of the river and revenge motifs, and the effect they have on the narrative and characters.

5 Eliot sees childhood as a crucial, formative time. How does the portrayal of Maggie as a child help us to understand the behaviour of Maggie as a woman?

6 Women play a large part in this novel, even though they are often considered inferior by the male characters. What do you learn about Victorian attitudes to women from *The Mill on the Floss*?

7 Bob Jakin is a functional character in the book, and of a different class to Maggie. Despite this, the reader likes him. Explain how Eliot's writing makes him a likeable character.

8 Through the use of humour, the novel shows the ridiculous side of the Victorian attitudes and characters of Maggie's aunts. Explain how Eliot achieves this.

9 In many ways Lucy is a typical Victorian girl and a direct contrast to Maggie. Describe her role in the book and whether she is realistically portrayed by Eliot.

10 Is Maggie a victim of her own character or of her circumstances? Discuss.

PART FIVE

CULTURAL CONNECTIONS

BROADER PERSPECTIVES

Film and video versions You can broaden your understanding of the text by watching dramatisations, e.g. a film version of *The Mill on the Floss*, available on video. It will help you to picture the period and place the characters in their correct era. But read the book before watching the film so that you know what is left out. You will then be able to spot differences between the text and the film, and it is useful to think about why these changes were made, and which version you prefer.

Relationships to other texts George Eliot wrote several other books and it would probably be helpful to read another one. *Silas Marner* is short and straightforward and will give you further understanding of Eliot's style and ideas. Alternatively, *Middlemarch* is considered her best novel; it is long and complex but beautifully written. Both books are available in Penguin Classics and have been dramatised by the BBC.

Another way of exploring the text is to compare it to a twentieth-century book which tackles similar themes or presents similar characters, but in a different time and setting. *To Kill a Mockingbird* by Harper Lee connects well with *The Mill on the Floss*, they both:
- belong to the genre of **bildungsroman** (see Literary Terms)
- are set in small towns with fixed ideas
- focus on a clever young girl with an adored older brother
- take the theme of outsiders and prejudice
- criticise unjust judgements and people
- contain aunts who disapprove of unconventional behaviour

- use dialect and children's speech convincingly
- balance tragic and comic elements

The style and language are similar in many ways, as Harper Lee admired pre-twentieth-century literature, but they are narrated differently. See for yourself!

autobiographical based on the author's life

allusion brief reference to another text

atmosphere mood

authorial voice or **tone** the author writes in such a way as to voice his/her opinion directly to the reader

bildungsroman novel which follows the growth of a character from childhood looking at their experiences and development

cathartic release for strong feelings or emotions

chronological/chronology events in a story related in the order in which they occur

climactic reaching a high point or climax

dialect style of speaking particular to an area

dramatic irony the reader knows something that is hidden from a character

foreshadows similar to prophesying, hinting of the future

ironic/irony saying one thing but conveying a different meaning

melodramatic exaggerated and unrealistic

motif repeated theme or image which adds to the book's symbolic structure

narrative tension the way the plot makes the reader want to know what will happen next

omniscient narrator the author tells the story and knows all the facts and thoughts of the characters

pathos writing which evokes strong feelings of sorrow or pity

plot the events of the story

realism/realistic the attempt to make a book echo real life

satire attack on a character or idea through humour, similar to irony

symbolic/symbolism the use of one thing to represent another

theme an important idea explored in the text

TEST YOURSELF (Book One)

A 1 Mrs Tulliver *(Chapter 2)*
••• 2 Tom *(Chapter 5)*
3 Bob Jakin *(Chapter 6)*
4 Mr Tulliver *(Chapter 7)*
5 Maggie *(Chapter 2)*
6 Tom *(Chapter 4)*
7 Lucy *(Chapter 10)*
8 Mr Tulliver *(Chapter 12)*

TEST YOURSELF (Book Two)

A 1 Stelling *(Chapter 1)*
••• 2 Maggie *(Chapter 1)*
3 Tom *(Chapter 1)*
4 Philip *(Chapter 6)*
5 Stelling *(Chapter 1)*
6 Philip *(Chapter 3)*
7 Maggie *(Chapter 5)*
8 Tom *(Chapter 6)*

TEST YOURSELF (Book Three)

A 1 Tom *(Chapter 1)*
••• 2 Mrs Tulliver *(Chapter 3)*
3 Maggie *(Chapter 3)*

4 Mr Deane *(Chapter 5)*
5 Maggie *(Chapter 5)*
6 Bob Jakin *(Chapter 6)*
7 Mr Tulliver *(Chapter 9)*

TEST YOURSELF (Books Four and Five)

A 1 Bob Jakin *(Book Four, Chapter 3)*
••• 2 Mr Tulliver *(Book Four, Chapter 3)*
3 Philip *(Book Five, Chapter 1)*
4 Tom *(Book Five, Chapter 5)*
5 Maggie *(Book Five, Chapter 1)*
6 Lucy *(Book Five, Chapter 4)*
7 Philip *(Book Five, Chapter 4)*
8 Mr Tulliver *(Book Five, Chapter 7)*

TEST YOURSELF (Books Six and Seven)

A 1 Lucy *(Book Six, Chapter 3)*
••• 2 Tom *(Book Six, Chapter 4)*
3 Wakem *(Book Six, Chapter 8)*
4 Stephen *(Book Six, Chapter 14)*
5 Stephen *(Book Six, Chapter 1)*
6 Maggie *(Book Six, Chapter 2)*
7 Tom *(Book Seven, Chapter 1)*
8 Stephen *(Book Seven, Chapter 4)*

NOTES

NOTES

NOTES

NOTES

NOTES

NOTES

OTHER TITLES

GCSE and equivalent levels (£3.50 each)

Maya Angelou
I Know Why the Caged Bird Sings

Jane Austen
Pride and Prejudice

Alan Ayckbourn
Absent Friends

Elizabeth Barrett Browning
Selected Poems

Robert Bolt
A Man for All Seasons

Harold Brighouse
Hobson's Choice

Charlotte Brontë
Jane Eyre

Emily Brontë
Wuthering Heights

Shelagh Delaney
A Taste of Honey

Charles Dickens
David Copperfield

Charles Dickens
Great Expectations

Charles Dickens
Hard Times

Charles Dickens
Oliver Twist

Roddy Doyle
Paddy Clarke Ha Ha Ha

George Eliot
Silas Marner

George Eliot
The Mill on the Floss

William Golding
Lord of the Flies

Oliver Goldsmith
She Stoops To Conquer

Willis Hall
The Long and the Short and the Tall

Thomas Hardy
Far from the Madding Crowd

Thomas Hardy
The Mayor of Casterbridge

Thomas Hardy
Tess of the d'Urbervilles

Thomas Hardy
The Withered Arm and other Wessex Tales

L.P. Hartley
The Go-Between

Seamus Heaney
Selected Poems

Susan Hill
I'm the King of the Castle

Barry Hines
A Kestrel for a Knave

Louise Lawrence
Children of the Dust

Harper Lee
To Kill a Mockingbird

Laurie Lee
Cider with Rosie

Arthur Miller
The Crucible

Arthur Miller
A View from the Bridge

Robert O'Brien
Z for Zachariah

Frank O'Connor
My Oedipus Complex and other stories

George Orwell
Animal Farm

J.B. Priestley
An Inspector Calls

Willy Russell
Educating Rita

Willy Russell
Our Day Out

J.D. Salinger
The Catcher in the Rye

William Shakespeare
Henry IV Part 1

William Shakespeare
Henry V

William Shakespeare
Julius Caesar

William Shakespeare
Macbeth

William Shakespeare
The Merchant of Venice

William Shakespeare
A Midsummer Night's Dream

William Shakespeare
Much Ado About Nothing

William Shakespeare
Romeo and Juliet

William Shakespeare
The Tempest

William Shakespeare
Twelfth Night

George Bernard Shaw
Pygmalion

Mary Shelley
Frankenstein

R.C. Sherriff
Journey's End

Rukshana Smith
Salt on the snow

John Steinbeck
Of Mice and Men

Robert Louis Stevenson
Dr Jekyll and Mr Hyde

Jonathan Swift
Gulliver's Travels

Robert Swindells
Daz 4 Zoe

Mildred D. Taylor
Roll of Thunder, Hear My Cry

Mark Twain
Huckleberry Finn

James Watson
Talking in Whispers

William Wordsworth
Selected Poems

A Choice of Poets

Mystery Stories of the Nineteenth Century including The Signalman

Nineteenth Century Short Stories

Poetry of the First World War

Six Women Poets

ADVANCED LEVEL TITLES

York Notes Advanced (£3.99 each)

Margaret Atwood
The Handmaid's Tale

Jane Austen
Mansfield Park

Jane Austen
Persuasion

Jane Austen
Pride and Prejudice

Alan Bennett
Talking Heads

William Blake
Songs of Innocence and of Experience

Charlotte Brontë
Jane Eyre

Emily Brontë
Wuthering Heights

Geoffrey Chaucer
The Franklin's Tale

Geoffrey Chaucer
General Prologue to the Canterbury Tales

Geoffrey Chaucer
The Wife of Bath's Prologue and Tale

Joseph Conrad
Heart of Darkness

Charles Dickens
Great Expectations

John Donne
Selected Poems

George Eliot
The Mill on the Floss

F. Scott Fitzgerald
The Great Gatsby

E.M. Forster
A Passage to India

Brian Friel
Translations

Thomas Hardy
The Mayor of Casterbridge

Thomas Hardy
Tess of the d'Urbervilles

Seamus Heaney
Selected Poems from Opened Ground

Nathaniel Hawthorne
The Scarlet Letter

James Joyce
Dubliners

John Keats
Selected Poems

Christopher Marlowe
Doctor Faustus

Arthur Miller
Death of a Salesman

Toni Morrison
Beloved

William Shakespeare
Antony and Cleopatra

William Shakespeare
As You Like It

William Shakespeare
Hamlet

William Shakespeare
King Lear

William Shakespeare
Measure for Measure

William Shakespeare
The Merchant of Venice

William Shakespeare
Much Ado About Nothing

William Shakespeare
Othello

William Shakespeare
Romeo and Juliet

William Shakespeare
The Tempest

William Shakespeare
The Winter's Tale

Mary Shelley
Frankenstein

Alice Walker
The Color Purple

Oscar Wilde
The Importance of Being Earnest

Tennessee Williams
A Streetcar Named Desire

John Webster
The Duchess of Malfi

W.B. Yeats
Selected Poems

FUTURE TITLES IN THE YORK NOTES SERIES

Chinua Achebe
Things Fall Apart

Edward Albee
Who's Afraid of Virginia Woolf?

Margaret Atwood
Cat's Eye

Jane Austen
Emma

Jane Austen
Northanger Abbey

Jane Austen
Sense and Sensibility

Samuel Beckett
Waiting for Godot

Robert Browning
Selected Poems

Robert Burns
Selected Poems

Angela Carter
Nights at the Circus

Geoffrey Chaucer
The Merchant's Tale

Geoffrey Chaucer
The Miller's Tale

Geoffrey Chaucer
The Nun's Priest's Tale

Samuel Taylor Coleridge
Selected Poems

Daniel Defoe
Moll Flanders

Daniel Defoe
Robinson Crusoe

Charles Dickens
Bleak House

Charles Dickens
Hard Times

Emily Dickinson
Selected Poems

Carol Ann Duffy
Selected Poems

George Eliot
Middlemarch

T.S. Eliot
The Waste Land

T.S. Eliot
Selected Poems

Henry Fielding
Joseph Andrews

E.M. Forster
Howards End

John Fowles
The French Lieutenant's Woman

Robert Frost
Selected Poems

Elizabeth Gaskell
North and South

Stella Gibbons
Cold Comfort Farm

Graham Greene
Brighton Rock

Thomas Hardy
Jude the Obscure

Thomas Hardy
Selected Poems

Joseph Heller
Catch-22

Homer
The Iliad

Homer
The Odyssey

Gerard Manley Hopkins
Selected Poems

Aldous Huxley
Brave New World

Kazuo Ishiguro
The Remains of the Day

Ben Jonson
The Alchemist

Ben Jonson
Volpone

James Joyce
A Portrait of the Artist as a Young Man

Philip Larkin
Selected Poems

D.H. Lawrence
The Rainbow

D.H. Lawrence
Selected Stories

D.H. Lawrence
Sons and Lovers

D.H. Lawrence
Women in Love

John Milton
Paradise Lost Bks I & II

John Milton
Paradise Lost Bks IV & IX

Thomas More
Utopia

Sean O'Casey
Juno and the Paycock

George Orwell
Nineteen Eighty-four

John Osborne
Look Back in Anger

Wilfred Owen
Selected Poems

Sylvia Plath
Selected Poems

Alexander Pope
Rape of the Lock and other poems

Ruth Prawer Jhabvala
Heat and Dust

Jean Rhys
Wide Sargasso Sea

William Shakespeare
As You Like It

William Shakespeare
Coriolanus

William Shakespeare
Henry IV Pt 1

William Shakespeare
Henry V

William Shakespeare
Julius Caesar

William Shakespeare
Macbeth

William Shakespeare
Measure for Measure

William Shakespeare
A Midsummer Night's Dream

William Shakespeare
Richard II

William Shakespeare
Richard III

William Shakespeare
Sonnets

William Shakespeare
The Taming of the Shrew

William Shakespeare
Twelfth Night

William Shakespeare
The Winter's Tale

George Bernard Shaw
Arms and the Man

George Bernard Shaw
Saint Joan

Muriel Spark
The Prime of Miss Jean Brodie

John Steinbeck
The Grapes of Wrath

John Steinbeck
The Pearl

Tom Stoppard
Arcadia

Tom Stoppard
Rosencrantz and Guildenstern are Dead

Jonathan Swift
Gulliver's Travels and The Modest Proposal

Alfred, Lord Tennyson
Selected Poems

W.M. Thackeray
Vanity Fair

Virgil
The Aeneid

Edith Wharton
The Age of Innocence

Tennessee Williams
Cat on a Hot Tin Roof

Tennessee Williams
The Glass Menagerie

Virginia Woolf
Mrs Dalloway

Virginia Woolf
To the Lighthouse

William Wordsworth
Selected Poems

Metaphysical Poets

York Notes – the Ultimate Literature Guides

York Notes are recognised as the best literature study guides.
If you have enjoyed using this book and have found it useful, you
can now order others directly from us – simply follow the ordering
instructions below.

HOW TO ORDER

Decide which title(s) you require and then order in one of the following
ways:

Booksellers
All titles available from good bookstores.

By post
List the title(s) you require in the space provided overleaf,
select your method of payment, complete your name and
address details and return your completed order form and
payment to:
>
> *Addison Wesley Longman Ltd*
> *PO BOX 88*
> *Harlow*
> *Essex CM19 5SR*

By phone
Call our Customer Information Centre on 01279 623923 to
place your order, quoting mail number: HEYN1.

By fax
Complete the order form overleaf, ensuring you fill in your
name and address details and method of payment, and fax it
to us on 01279 414130.

By e-mail
E-mail your order to us on awlhe.orders@awl.co.uk listing
title(s) and quantity required and providing full name and
address details as requested overleaf. Please quote mail
number: HEYN1. Please do not send credit card details by
e-mail.

York Notes Order Form

Titles required:

Quantity	Title/ISBN	Price

Sub total _____

Please add £2.50 postage & packing _____

(P & P is free for orders over £50) _____

Total _____

Mail no: HEYN1

Your Name _____

Your Address _____

_____

Postcode _____ Telephone _____

Method of payment

☐ I enclose a cheque or a P/O for £_____ made payable to Addison Wesley Longman Ltd

☐ Please charge my Visa/Access/AMEX/Diners Club card
Number _____ Expiry Date _____
Signature _____ Date _____

(please ensure that the address given above is the same as for your credit card)

Prices and other details are correct at time of going to press but may change without notice. All orders are subject to status.

☐ *Please tick this box if you would like a complete listing of Longman Study Guides (suitable for GCSE and A-level students)*

York Press

Longman

Addison Wesley Longman